Elizabeth Hamill

Sunbeams in the Mist

A COLLECTION OF POETRY & STORIES,
CELEBRATING GOD AND HIS CREATION

SUNBEAMS IN THE MIST

Copyright © 2018 Elizabeth Hamill

ISBN:978-1-9997955-1-1

All rights reserved.
No part of this publication may be reproduced, stored in a retrieval system, or transmitted in any form or by any means, electronic, mechanical, photocopying or otherwise, without prior written consent of the publisher except as provided by under United Kingdom copyright law. Short extracts may be used for review purposes with credits given.

All Scriptures quoted are taken from New International Version, except where stated.
THE HOLY BIBLE, NEW INTERNATIONAL VERSION®, NIV®
Copyright © 1973, 1978, 1984, 2011 by Biblica, Inc.®
Used by permission. All rights reserved worldwide.

Published by
Maurice Wylie Media
Bethel Media House
Tobermore
Magherafelt,
Northern Ireland
BT45 5SG (UK)

Publishers' statement: *Throughout this book the love for our God is such that whenever we refer to Him we honour with Capitals. On the other hand, when referring to the devil, we refuse to acknowledge him with any honour to the point of violating grammatical rule and withholding a capital.*

www.MauriceWylieMedia.com

PLACING MINISTRY ONTO PAPER

Create | Brand | Establish

Contents

Endorsement	9
Foreword	11
Story I The Annual Visit	**13**
Poem – Paper Maps	15
Poem – Being There	18
Story II The Night Shift	**20**
Poem – Wit's End Corner	23
Poem – Look Up	25
Story III A Winter's Tale	**27**
Poem – The Night Queen	30
Story IV The Intellectual	**33**
Poem – Morning Glory	35
Poem – Waiting	37
Story V Cobblestones Streets	**39**
Poem – The Little Lost Lamb	41
Story VI Ripples in a Fountain	**45**
Poem – The Quiet Man	47
Story VII Strange Bedfellows	**50**
Story VIII Urban Nights	**53**
Poem – Countdown	56
Poem – This Man	58

Story IX Contentment   61
Poem – Heavenly Light   63

Story X The Tears of God   65
Poem – Soul Music   68
Poem – Apathy   70
Poem – Again   71
Poem – No Copyrights   73

Story XI Backward Glances   75
Chapter One: Trunks and Secrets   75
Chapter Two: An Unexpected Trip   84
Chapter Three: Countryside   91

PERCEPTION

Poem – Moving On   106

Story XII Woolly Friend's   109

Story XIII The Birthday Party   113

ANTICPATION

Story XIV A Worried Man   116

Story XV A Landlord's Dilemma   119

Story XVI Promise and Joy   122
Poem – The Travellers   124

Story XVII The Eyes of a King   127

HEALING WORDS

Poem – Alive Again	132
Poem – Bartimaeus	135
Poem – Reaching Out	138
Poem – Life Water	141
Poem – Changed Ways	144
Poem – Empty Nets	147
Poem – Peace	150

VOICES AROUND THE CROSS

Poem – The Old Misfit	152
Poem – The Soldier	155
Poem – Freedom Day	157
Poem – The Donkey's Tale	160

MEMORIES

Poem – Evening Shadows	163
Poem – Broken Friendship	166
Poem – A Sleepless Night	168
Poem – Sweet Wine	172
Poem – Leave Taking	175
Poem – Treasure	178

JOY

Poem – First Light	182
Poem – Hasty Words	185
Poem – I Give Thanks	188

Endorsement

What is the capacity of the human heart? My medical friends tell me that on average the heart can contain 10 fl. oz. But the capacity of the human heart is much more than just mechanical and physical. Scripture describes the heart as the core the very centre of a person.

This book of Elizabeth's shows us more of the capacity of the human heart. Over many years of reflection, prayer and worship, she has collected observations of the joy and pain of life. The wonder and power of the natural world and how all of these can signpost us to the power and purposes of Almighty God. Elizabeth stands in a long historic line of individuals, who have found a place in words, a way to share and give shape to their place in life, and before God.

As Elizabeth shares what God has put in her heart, my prayer is that many will be encouraged to open their hearts to the saving grace of Almighty God.

'Blessed are the pure in heart, for they shall see God.' Matthew 5:8.

Canon Mark McConnell

Rector, St. Patrick's Church, Ballymena

Foreword

I have had the privilege of sharing in Elizabeth Hamill's faith journey as her minister over nearly 30 years. Her faith was forged through many challenges in her life, and as with Jacob, through some "wrestling" with God. That faith held her and in a quiet way infused her life. I came to value her as a companion on the journey, a person who encouraged an open heart and who was both perceptive and supportive.

Over many years she has been a member of a church study group in which I participated. As the members explored Scripture she always manages to bring fresh insights to passages and to ground these insights in everyday life. Her openness and honesty would at times surprise us but at the same time inspire others and build fellowship.

Humble by nature, not many knew of her gift with words and her ability to write poetry and stories. She loved to express herself in this way and over the years built up quite a body of work. Slow to acknowledge her skill with words and to use these words to paint pictures and create atmosphere, occasionally I did persuade her to share some of her work in the context of worship. I especially remember her poems/stories bringing to life some of those caught up in the ministry of Jesus. These offerings did contribute to the worship and touch lives – but only a limited number was exposed to her work.

Now with this publication, many more can come to appreciate and enjoy her work. My prayer is that those who engage with this book will be encouraged further along the path of faith. May what Elizabeth has gifted to us be a blessing to many.

Canon Stuart Lloyd

Retired Rector, St Patrick's Church, Ballymena

Story 1

The Annual Visit

The hammer beat loudly on the bell of the alarm clock, waking me from my dreams. As I reached out and pressed the tiny lever that cut off the noise, the icy cold air jumped on my hand like a lion pouncing on its prey.

I dreaded winter mornings, especially those that began at 5am. I snuggled back into the warmth of the soft feather bed for a few more precious minutes. With great courage, I threw back the blankets and braved the cold. As my feet touched the floorboards, shivers coursed like iced water through my body. My teeth seemed to have a will of their own as they chattered against each other.

The still bright moon shone through the small attic window allowing me just enough light to find the matches and bring the candle to life. The soft yellow glow was comforting.

Downstairs I heard noises. Mother was up and about. I took my dress and other items of clothing from beneath the mattress and put them on quickly; with my cold breath I blew the candle out and hurried down into the kitchen.

The small fire of sticks was crackling in the old stove and the kettle was starting to steam. The oil lamp flickered and spluttered, reminding me that it needed a new wick. My mother worked quietly at the table. Sadness spread through me as I watched her spread the margarine thinly on the bread and wrap it in brown paper, I knew she would eat less at dinnertime so I could have an extra slice.

The first low moan of the factory horn sounded as I closed the front door behind me. I drew my shawl tighter around my shoulders and joined the trail of mill workers coming down the hill, the women like me, had their long shawls wrapped around them like a second skin. The men felt the icy cold too, their hands were pushed deep into the pockets of ragged coats; their faces were almost hidden from view by thick knitted mufflers and cloth caps. The steady trampling of feet on the cobblestones the only sound. We moved along the road like worker ants.

The tall iron gates of the factory were wide open. In the glimmer of the gaslight they reminded me of Noah's Ark and us the chosen animals. Some mornings I used to imagine the gates were a great gaping mouth that swallowed us whole and then at the home time horn, spat us out again. I shivered at my thoughts.

"Are you starting work today, or tomorrow, Mary Jackson?"

The loud harsh voice of the doffing mistress boomed in my ears. I looked up into her puffed red face.

"Sorry, miss," I mumbled as I quickly kicked off my shoes and tied a course apron over my dress. I kept myself busy that day in fear of the mistress reporting me. Jobs were hard to find and my small contribution to my mother each week was needed to keep us from the workhouse.

Tomorrow I could dream all I wanted. Tomorrow I could stand beside my lavender smelling school teacher and hear about all the wonderful places in the world, but today was a working day for the likes of me.

Tomorrow I could be a schoolgirl again, but today and every other day, I was a worker, or as the mistress often called me *'just a lazy half timer'.*

I closed the photograph album. This was my annual visit to the places of my childhood, and each time I opened it, the memories became clear in my mind. Slowly the loud cross voice of the doffing mistress faded from my ears.

The factory is closed and the looms are silent. Carefully I set my `*yesterday's*` back on the shelf and looked around my cosy warm room. Outside, the dusky grey of evening was fast approaching. I walked over and put on the electric light. I smiled to myself each time I switched it on. Electricity, to me was a wonderful invention. The expression *'the good old days'* came to mind, I smiled again in the knowledge that only the rich people of sixty or more years ago could have agreed with it. I for one found nothing good about freezing cold mornings, bare feet and not enough food.

After enjoying my cup of hot chocolate, I plumped up the pillows on my warm bed. "I suppose," I said, to my dear late husband's photo, "if I were really honest, I wouldn't swap or exchange one day of my childhood. If I had, you and I may never have met at the factory gates, but that, dear Albert is another story."

Paper maps...

We live in a fast-paced world and like it or not, the fastness rubs on to us. Time is so precious, we are either losing it, behind it, catching up on it or we've used it all up!

One thing we can't do is go back in time, physically. However, we can return to past events in our lives by way of memory. Instantly we can relive and smile at the good times and grimace at the not so good. Our memory acts like a book, each page contains events and happenings, many of us would like to bypass the pain-filled pages and if we could, erase them. But like all the rest of our memories, they are written in invisible, indelible ink. Photograph albums are on a different scale; we can remove photos with ease and forget we ever took them. An empty space, the only evidence they ever existed.

My grandmother died about forty years ago. In the process of clearing out the contents of her home, we found an old dusty photo album. The brown-tinged photos were of her friends and past events. Happy and solemn faces, each with a voice that we couldn't hear. There was no one to ask who, why or where and no scraps of writings or letters to help us trace the silent people in the photos. Many times as a family we all said; "If only she was here…"

There is another book of memories, it doesn't have tangible photos, but it describes in detail our world from creation. The Old and New Testament are both combined as one, the book is the Bible. In it we find recollections that give us a mental picture of life and living more than two thousand years ago. Within its pages we meet marvellous people, the most wonderful one being Jesus Christ, God's only Son.

Talking creates memories. Many would say, talking is a waste of time. I disagree; I am thankful the disciples and so many others talked and then recorded their memories for you and me. We don't need photographs, The Bible and every word in it is as alive today as on the day it was chronicled.

Perhaps you know of someone who would like to talk about their life. '**Paper Maps**' might remind you to `waste a little time` for someone and their memories.

Paper Maps...

High up on the dresser shelf
Amid cobwebs and broken delft,
My grandmother's photo album lay
Forgotten since she passed away.

Blowing dust clouds in the air
I eased it down with gentle care,
With misty eyes I took a look
Inside her much-loved memory book.

Photographs tinged brown with time
Of people she could bring to mind,
High buttoned boots, long plaited hair
And bicycles that two can share.

Paper maps…

The faded pictures told of bonds
With faces from the past long gone,
School friends that carried chalk and slate
Scratched on each a name and date.

I turned a page and she was there
In wedding gown and ringlets fair,
Beside her stood a tall young man
With smiling eyes and whiskers grand.

Another page I turned with care
To see a child with curly hair,
Holding tight within his arms
A tiny new-born baby lamb.

Grandmother's book of photographs
Her life set out in paper maps,
Tracing her time upon the earth
Her time in time before my birth.

Wiping tears I closed the book
Remembering my small kitchen nook,
I had a shelf with room to spare,
Her memories now with mine would share.

A treasure found, now sits in state
With cockle shells and china plates,
A jewel reflecting and bringing light
Grandmother's book, of imaged life.

Being there...

All of us, at one time or another want something we can't have. When I was a child I wanted a special doll for Christmas. I wrote notes every week from Halloween until Christmas Eve. My grandmother would, as was the custom, post my pleading letters up the chimney to Santa!

Christmas morning arrived, my stocking was there, filled with an apple, orange, knitted mitts and a silver threepenny bit, but no special doll. There was a doll; it sat beneath the tree like someone that had just been in a bad accident! It had scratches on its face and a chipped thumb! I looked again but said nothing.

My grandmother said, "There's a note attached." I pulled the sad looking doll from beneath the tree and reached her the note. She read, "This is a very sick doll, would you give her a home?" I looked again at the doll; waited a few minutes, then went and fetched my blue crochet blanket. "This will help her," I said as I wrapped the doll up tightly. I grew to love that doll. She was unique, with a bandaged hand and a sticking plaster on her face. My friends said I had a ready-made patient for when we played hospitals!

Many years later my grandmother was staying with us over the Christmas period. On Christmas morning everyone was excited, especially my daughter, "I got my doll!" She shouted as she jumped around like a jelly bean. The delight on her face delighted me. After lunch as my grandmother and I sat in the quiet kitchen, she told me about that Christmas so long ago. She said money was so scarce that she couldn't afford a small doll let alone the one I wanted. She said she bought the doll for a few pennies at a jumble sale and wrote the note. I loved my grandmother and that Christmas I loved her a million times more. As we talked I really found out just how hard those times were for her and many others. She was always there for me and until she died, I was always there for her.

It's so comforting to think of our Heavenly Father being there for each and every one of us. We may be grown-up, but in His eyes we are His children.

Being There...

It's being there, just being there, to show how much you love and care
To offer help to overcome the growing pains of being young,
By being there…

It's being there to share their life, in happy days or nights of strife
To touch their heart with gentleness
and ease away their restlessness,
By being there…

It's being there as they stand tall and reach beyond childhood halls
There to guide and help amend,
hurt caused by many so-called friends,
By being there…

It's being there when showers come,
when they can't see the hiding sun
There to quell the many fears or ease away the hurting tears,
By being there…

It's being there as dreams come true, as they step out in lofty shoes
To conquer all with mighty plans,
unseen by them the sinking sand,
By being there…

It's being there to always care, the way you did when unborn fair
Beneath your beating heart did sleep,
then as now for them you weep,
By being there…

It's being there till your last breath,
with loving care and tenderness
There to guide along life's way, to love and bless them all their days,
By being there.

Story 11

The Night Shift

The overfilled kettle bubbled as it hung on the crook. Every so often a few drops of water escaped from its spout and fell on the hot coals. I opened one eye as I heard hissing and spitting for the umpteenth time.

Just as I was thinking of moving to somewhere less noisy, the kettle was taken from the crook and set on the hearth. I dozed again, but once more I was disturbed, this time, by the ear-splitting strikes of the hall clock.

Feeling disgruntled I moved to the empty armchair in the corner of the kitchen. All I needed was a few hours of sleep before I started my work. When I did waken, everyone had gone to bed and the room was in total darkness.

Reluctantly, I left the comfort of the chair and washed my face quickly, revived myself with a drink of milk and slipped out the back door. It was a beautiful night. The sight of the moon hanging in the sky like a giant silver ball made me gasp. I kept glancing up at it as I dallied along the lane listening to the sound of rustling leaves and the occasional eerie hoot of an owl.

A few minutes later I stopped to check the cows in the bottom field. They were asleep in one corner, their breath coming in great clouds of steam - perhaps this was their idea of a Turkish bath. I hurried on towards the cornfield. From there I could take a short cut to one of my favourite spots, the river.

The tow path was deserted. I paused a moment to gaze at the water. The reflection of the moon had turned it into a long slow moving mirror. The sight was magical. Close to the bank, almost hidden in the reeds, I spotted a family of swans. They sat motionless. I slipped past them remembering the old saying 'let sleeping dogs lie' or in this case, swans! I took another sneaky look at them before making my way along the path toward the small wooden fence beside the old stone bridge.

I stood on the bridge for a moment; then I completed my nightly workout of jumping the fence, followed by a two-hundred-yard dash across the meadow to the old disused railway yard. Everyone knows that athletes need to rest after exercise and I had just settled myself in the long grass, near the old rusty engine, when I spotted the stranger.

It was his tattered coat and eyes that darted every way that made me suspicious of him. I started to edge closer to get a better look at him when my foot snapped a twig. I froze, but the stranger had heard the crack. He looked around and then took off like a young stallion. I charged after him but gave up when I saw him leap the fence and race into a clump of trees. I felt like an old carthorse as I lay on the cold grass, exhausted and out of breath.

My thumping heart seemed in no hurry to return to its normal pace. When it eventually did, I made a mental note to come to work earlier tomorrow night, just in case the stranger dared to make another appearance. My strength was fully restored as I strolled across a hay field, jumped another turnstile and finally reached the crossroads.

After I had checked that everything was as it should be in the adjoining fields, I settled down for another rest on an upturned milk crate. How I loved the countryside and my work. Only those who work the night shift can appreciate the quietness and peace that comes in the midnight hours. I felt like a contented king. I sat on my makeshift throne until the black velvet sky started to slowly change to grey. I knew that soon the greyness would disappear as dawn appeared with its first shafts of golden light. I felt privileged to witness the dawning of a new day. I've often wondered why most people prefer their bed to this marvellous sight.

Cutting into my thoughts and the stillness, came six strikes of the village clock, then I heard the first loud crowing of an early morning rooster. The long night hours had passed quickly and the sounds I'd heard over the past few minutes told me my work was almost over for another night.

A warm feeling of contentment spread through me as I took a last look around at my peaceful sleeping world. I was foot sore and weary by the time I reached the back door of our house. I slipped in quietly, the welcoming glow from the fire a cheering sight. I sat for a few minutes and warmed myself at the red mountain of coal, then made my way across the kitchen as delicious smells came to my nose. All I wanted now was some breakfast and about six hours undisturbed sleep.

"You look tired this morning. Had a busy night?" Mary asked as she set my breakfast beside me. I rubbed my nose on her soft dressing gown. She gave my ear a comforting rub, then cuddled me gently in her arms. I loved my early morning cuddle. It made me feel very special. Ten minutes later as I crept into bed, I wondered if everyone that worked the night shift came home to a good breakfast and a cuddle.

"*Yes Tom*", I said to myself as my eyelids met. "*You are a very fortunate cat indeed!*"

Wit's end corner...

Ten years ago, I knew a young man who went on a short trip, a trip that turned into a journey, a journey that lasted for just a few months. This youth was a slave to drugs, an addiction that took him far from his family, work and a respectable life. Help in many forms were offered, but the pull of his dependence defeated the need to be free. It was with sadness I attended his funeral.

I myself stepped onto one of life's roller coaster rides. It halted at Easter time six months later. My journey was caused by the death of my son. I journeyed to a place in my mind that was hideous. I kept everyone at arm's length. I was unreachable. I felt lost, alone and abandoned by God. No one could help or reach me as I sunk deeper into a black pit. I was alone and battling with an unseen enemy.

There are many pathways in life that lead to despair. Drug addictions, divorce, redundancy, illness, death of a loved one, are just a few. Depression is not like a common cold, there are no visible signs; it happens without warning. It creeps slowly and steadily like thick black slime and blocks the light from entering our once coherent thoughts. We enter an isolated room without doors.

Support is there in many forms, but it takes strength to reach out and receive it. Accepting help by way of medication or physicians, who understood the mysteries of reason, brought my journey to an end. If you or someone you know is suffering depression, please seek and accept the help offered.

The darkness of dejection had crushed my faith and trust in God. That Easter I reached out in faith, my God was there, waiting to enfold me in His loving arms… My God was always there, He had never left my side.

Wit's End Corner…

I remember that day…
My life road became misty, so very unclear
When it started to bend I started to fear,
All paths kept winding like snakes on a tree
Troubles kept coming, not in ones but in threes.

People said, "Things will get better and fall into place"
'When?' I wanted to scream and shout in their face,
I'd been confused day after day
But no one could help or show me the way.

Others said; "All things come to an end"
Just around the next corner, just beyond the next bend,
You'll find sunshine, instead of cold rain"
I turned away, too tired to explain.

I could go no further, I'd run out of road
The signposts of life seemed to laugh, jeer and goad,
`You stand on your own with no help from your friends
You've reached the corner, it's called *Wit's End*.`

I was lost, lost in a life, a life without sun
With days and nights all merging as one,
Then came the voices, some of them said
'End it all… things will be better, once you are dead.'

Quietly through the mist of the heartache and tears
Another voice came to my ears,
'Child, I remember when you held my hand,
When you trusted in me, child… I'm waiting and I understand.'

I walked away from that corner, the Lord by my side
My hand in His letting Him be my guide,
And He's always there, in the day or the night
Watching and waiting with his guiding light.

If you walk down the road of despair and defeat
And come to that corner where roads criss-cross and meet,
It's there you'll find Jesus, He waits for you to reach out your hand
Jesus, God's Son, waits to enfold you in His loving arms.

Look up

If someone slapped you a few times on your face, you would agree that you end up with a red face. There is another type of slap but it doesn't leave any visual evidence. These marks are inflicted on your heart and mind. The slap goes under the names of verbal/mental abuse.

Some people might have experienced verbal abuse as children, in a relationship, during high school, in college, the home where they now reside. This type of cruelty is kept hidden from family and friends; it can go on for decades, in or outside of the home. Both Christian and non-Christians are mentally and physically abused on a daily basis and accept it as being normal, by believing they are under the control of their husband, wife or family.

Mental and physical abuse is as old as time itself; we read in the Bible how Job's friends and his wife blamed him for his misfortune, Tamar was raped by her brother Amnon, King Saul verbally abused his son Jonathan, Delilah nagged Samson until he told her about his hair. There are many more examples…

In today's society people keep this type of cruelty hidden. It is not easy to defend yourself… the voice of doubt fills your mind, *will anyone believe this of my church going parents… my husband is influential in the town… I will bring shame to the family…* unless you speak, you are resigned to living a fear-filled existence.

When we are hurting we need to remember to '*look up*' to God and His healing light…

Look Up...

The rains came before nightfall and my beautiful flowers
That had danced and swayed to an unheard tune,
Now stood, heads bowed, forlorn, doomed
My sweet-smelling flowers, exposed to the pain
Of battering and bruising, from cold driving rain.

The long night passed and morning light came
With pale rays of sunshine appearing again,
I watched as my flowers raised their weary heads
Sweet flowers that by now should have been dead.

I watched as each head, turned from left and from right
Until all of them faced the bright beams of light,
Slowly, so slowly they all stood tall
Each petal head bright against my old garden wall.

Stronger and stronger each flower grew
All of them swaying to a tune they each knew,
My flowers were back, back to full life
Dancing in the warmth of golden sunlight.

Sometimes, our lives are just like the flowers
We get battered and bruised from life's heavy showers,
We struggle with living and the downpour of pain
Till our hearts are crushed, broken and maimed.

It's then a voice, like the warmth of the sun
Whispers 'lift your eyes, look up precious one,
Look up to my light, to me only yield
Stand tall in my strength… for I am your shield.'

STORY 111

A Winter's Tale

I had just entered the bell tower when I heard the sound. The unmistakable click-clicking of high-heeled shoes. I knew that they could only belong to Mrs Gracie.

I moved to the window. As usual the bright red three-inch heels were working overtime in an attempt to support a pair of balloon ankles and a ton of pride.

Mrs Gracie still lived in the sixties, unlike her daughter Gloria who plodded along in a pair of boots that were sensible for this type of weather but would have been more at home on a building site. Gloria was the youngest of Mrs Gracie's daughters and was the trendiest person anyone could wish to meet, with her multi-pierced ears and hair that changed colour every two weeks.

Mrs Gracie was in my estimation the last of the die-hards or rather the fall-hards. I was busy chomping on a barley-sugar sweet when I heard the commotion. The spindly heels and the hidden patch of ice were arguing. The ice won. Once more pride lay sprawled on the path.

I'm happy to say that no damage was done to the unfortunate woman due to the thickness of an ancient fur coat and a well-padded posterior. A few minutes later Mrs Gracie's calamity was history, the reason, more sounds. Scuffling and scraping came from behind the ramshackle cupboard. I knew the culprits. It was a nightly ritual for the cheeky Presbyterian mice from across the road. Sometimes, just sometimes I felt sorry for the hungry thieves as I chased them back to their home ground.

I waited a few seconds then rattled an empty cola tin, and then the sprint for the open door was on. As I left the tower I glanced at the dog-eared notice: 'No food or drink - mice about.'

What's needed here, I thought, were a few dead mice tied to the ropes! Of course, I dismissed the thought immediately! It was a nice thought, nicer still would be the yells and squeals from the bell-ringers!

My next port of call was the overlarge fir tree that grew two feet from the church door. It needed a shake. Just as I reached the door, the strains of *The First Noel* came seeping through the very large keyhole. Someone had removed the key. I knew an icy draft would be sweeping over the pews. The end result would be stiff necks and sore ears arriving with the turkey and sprouts.

I made a mental note of the empty keyhole as I gave the tree another shake. The loud peal of the bells made me jump. The service was over and the ringers were pulling with gusto. It must have been the extra glass of mulled wine they indulged in before taking up the ropes.

Slowly it came, another sound, a sound that could be cured with a few drops or perhaps a large can of oil - the long-drawn-out creaking of the church door. Another note for the list. I pulled myself together and focused my attention on the now wide-open door in front of me. I had a clear view of all the regulars.

Mrs Gracie, as usual, after her annual fall was being fussed over by everyone. Her rouged cheeks were growing redder as she decided whose arm to take to guide her to the car park. She finally settled on the arm of the local publican, after he told her a hot-toddy would set her to rights.

Clever woman! One after another the congregation filtered through the door. The rectors repeated 'good evening', sounded like a gramophone with a sticky needle. I watched him, or rather I watched the drip at the end of his nose. Will it or won't it fall? I waited with bated breath and then, just when I thought it would happen, he sniffed.

My eyes, at that point, reluctantly left his nose and travelled down to his feet. I often wonder if the cold weather made him more forgetful than usual. But then, the Rector is a bit woolly-headed in more ways than one. The church wardens used to tut-tut at his bicycle clips still in place under his cassock, and everyone could see them when he served communion.

The present curate has also picked up some of the rector's strange ways. In the summer, and sometimes the winter, he wears open-toed sandals without socks! I could say a lot more, but as the saying goes, the less said…

Fifteen minutes later the rector closed the large door behind him. I watched as he drove away in a cloud of exhaust fumes. It was only then that the thought struck me - why does he wear bicycle clips when driving the car? I was still thinking about the clips when a delicious smell wafted over my nose. The supper was about to be served in the gatehouse.

As I plodded through the snow to the back door, my thoughts were on the days ahead. Christmas week is always busy and so many things can go wrong. The ropes in the bell tower would have to be checked and the crib would have to be retrieved from below the stage in the main hall. As usual, the annual hunt for Joseph's head will bring panic. The donations of flowers will again bring more headaches for the fussy members of the Mothers' Union. I've often wondered how deciding on which vase of holly goes where can be so difficult. If they had to contend with all the problems of a caretaker I could understand.

I shook the snow from my feet and entered the kitchen. The sound of the logs spitting and cracking in the big open fireplace, their woody smell and the aroma of sausages was a delight to the nose. I moved over to the fireplace and did as all men do. I warmed my legs, front and back!

After supper I slumped down in my favourite armchair. Before my eyes closed, my thoughts returned to all that had happened this evening and to all the mishaps that would take place before Christmas Day.

It was at that moment Eddie switched on the radio, and the strains of '*One Day at a Time*' drifted to my half-closed ears. Yes, I thought, all a junior caretaker can do is take one day or night at a time.

I was almost asleep when my boss called me.

"Murphy, do you want another sausage?" I left the chair in a flash.

"This job has the nicest perks," I said to myself as a large juicy sausage was placed on my plate. Before I tucked in to my extras, I showed my good manners and thanks, by way of winding my long black tail around Eddie's trouser leg, and of course I purred ever so loudly…

The Night Queen…

When I was a child, street lights were few and far between. Travelling on foot at night was eerie, the fortunate few carried a torch; we that didn't have that luxury depended on the moon.

In 1969, I saw the first photos of the moon's surface, the photos left me disappointed. The silvery ball was flawed. Those first blurred photos said it all, the moon was ugly. Years later I learned more about the surface of the moon and why it was so scarred.

In the Bible we read of people that were marred, people like Judas Iscariot, King Herod Antipas, Salome and Sheba, to name a few. All of them kept their flaws concealed from those around them. They were manipulative and conniving, everything they did was for their own pleasure or betterment.

In today's world it's no different. Unscrupulous people could be our neighbours, businesses or governments. It has taken time and years to blemish the moon's surface. Perhaps time and living in our fast-paced society causes flaws and blemishes in people too.

The Night Queen...

A regal queen on a dark-blue throne
Diamond draped she sits alone,
Her night attire a silvery gown
An entourage that sweeps the ground.

The pale night queen adorns the night
Serenely she waits in gossamer light,
Till she decides it's time to roam
And overview her vast kingdom.

Slowly she drifts by darkened pond
And gently strokes a sleeping swan,
Resting now on forest path
She hides as field mice scurry past.

Then turning quick at laughing hoot
She follows owls in night pursuit,
Then keeps company with a mole
Until she joins the cat patrol.

She lingers now to watch entranced
Bright fireflies in ritual dance,
Then sprightly darts within the trees
To play a game with shadow leaves.

Slowing pace she rests awhile
Beside a wooden man-made stile,
In the silence a loud cock crows
Reminding her it's time to go.

With paler face she leaves with grace
Other lands await her embrace,
As her kingdom stirs in the misty dawn
She disappears… she is gone.

Story IV

The Intellectual

I strolled into the garden. It was a perfect day. Golden beams of sunlight spilled out from a cloudless blue sky, then burst and scattered onto the carpet of rainbow-coloured flowers.

I stretched out on the rug and could only think of three words to describe everything - glorious, absolutely glorious. I felt at one with the world on this beautiful June morning.

Everyone was busy with all sorts of indoors tasks and I had the garden to myself. I knew exactly what I was going to do for the next hour. I was going to listen. In the normal course of a day I am quite active, but I insist on making time for the simple pleasures in life. If I had to draw up an inventory of my favourite pastimes, listening would be top of the list.

I think when one closes one's eyes and listens it's like going back to nature. No thoughts entered my head except for those three words - glorious, absolutely glorious.

Several hundred sounds started to slowly penetrate my ears. As usual the first sound belonged to the birds. Some sang sweetly while others chirped and squawked loudly. It was their way of scolding the visiting foreigners for landing on their territory. The beech tree at the bottom of the garden seemed to be in no mood for any impromptu landings either; its way of reprimand was to rustle its leaves every so often. I could quite understand, after all, who wants intruders on a day like this.

Another sound came from the foot of the garden. It was the water fountain. I listened to its soft tinkle, knowing in about two seconds its noise would change to a rushing gushing flow, as it splashed over the pink pebbles. Then when all its energy was spent, it would return to a tinkle. Ten minutes later it would repeat its cycle.

It's funny how certain sounds remind one of some people. I'm sure you've come across the type I'm talking about - always hurrying, always busy, but getting nowhere fast. I turned my head when I heard the footsteps. They belonged to a caterpillar that was inching its way across one of the large sunflower leaves. Who could miss hearing all those feet?

The next sound was a loud buzzing. It told me that the bumblebees were on patrol. I lay quietly as they flew around the garden like World War Two fighter pilots. After a few minutes the buzzing slowly faded as the black and yellow bombers crash-landed among the rhododendrons. The next sound I heard was nibbling. I knew, even with my eyes closed, that it was the two small mice that lived in the church across the road. They sneak over to our garden every day looking for food. I know there's a saying about church mice being poor, but really in this day and age…

I lay with my eyes closed tight, thinking about all the interesting sounds that most people never take time to listen to. Suddenly my thoughts were interrupted by a smell. Should I open my eyes and investigate, or should I ignore it? I decided to open my eyes. A minute later I was in the kitchen - that's where the smell came from.

By the way, the aroma that had me put aside my hearing sense so abruptly was roast chicken. It's good for the brain, so they say, or is it fish? I suppose it really doesn't matter, unless you're a vegetarian, in which case you won't like this smell, but I do. Roast chicken and gravy - glorious, absolutely glorious. It's just what an intellectual dog needs, after a morning of eavesdropping…

Morning Glory...

I'm sure you know of many people who are fanatical about their gardens. They love everyone to admire the perfection of the flowers and plants, but we can almost hear their unsaid words; 'Look but don't touch.' Nothing - cats, children, leaves from neighbouring trees, to name a few - are not allowed to touch.

One summer morning around 6am, I was wandering around what I call my garden, concrete slabs with a border of sweet pea, four roses and hundreds of nasturtiums! Most gardeners would wince at the sight. Suddenly breaking into my thoughts and through the morning mist came a beam of sunlight. It crept among the sleepy flowers, then without warning, more and more golden beams appeared. What fun those tiny rays of light had, as they touched flower after flower; shone like spotlights on the spiders and their silvery networks, or jumped out from behind the garden shed.

The scene being played out before me, reminded me of my children; the day I took all of them to a large toyshop. Running here and there, touching this and that and quickly developing the, *I wants!* I giggled to myself as I remembered the shop assistant's face. More giggles came when I thought of the many gardeners with their *look but don't touch* way of thinking. I wonder how far their eyebrows would rise if they could see the activity in their gardens in early morning, better still, what about the night visitors and the games they play during the hours of darkness. I must add, I have the highest regard for professional gardeners and their prize blooms. Horticulture in any form is a delight to look at, a bit like my apple pie, lovely to look at but nicer to eat! God welcomes us all into His garden and He never raises his eyebrows...

Morning Glory...

Evening mists that make no sound
Still asleep on tree and ground,
Soon with the dawn will slip away
As night concedes to waiting day.

Gentle rain like silver pearls
Trickle down from cloudy swirls,
Then pushing through the curls of grey
Beams of gold come out to play.

Sunbeams that stray within tall trees
Play peek-a-boo with all the leaves,
A game that turns them jewel bright
A canopy of dappled light.

Soft beams that touch a web of lace
Spun with care then laid in place,
Around a tiny petal head
A bonnet for a rose-bud red.

Evening mists that make no sound
Steal away from all around,
To leave the garden in the clutch
 Of sunbeams… and their golden touch.

Waiting...

The yearly job of clearing dead leaves, plants and flower heads from our once colourful gardens begins with the first frosts of winter. A few years ago in my modest garden, a single rose had survived the night frost, it stood proudly, almost defiant, until the next morning.

I had a friend who continually stated that he was not good enough and would wait and try to live a better life before becoming a Christian. Nothing would convince him that God wants us with all our imperfections.

During the last months of his earthly life my dear friend came to Jesus. Before he died he witnessed to many people, always ending his testimony with two words, *'Don't Wait.'*

So many people are like that one last rose in my garden, they hang on… and on… until the frost of winter appears.

Waiting...

  From rumpled beds and unused stays
  My garden called that autumn day,
To clean, to glean and set it free
From corpse that fell or tightly cleaved.

  I toiled till blue met twilight dark
With memories print on aching heart,
Sweet memories of perfumed air
And dancing heads that knew no care.

Then glancing up with tear-wet eye
I sensed her form seek evening sky,
Tightly wrapped in dark green shawl
Sheltering near the black stone wall.

Statuesque, delicate, refined
An alabaster face by time unlined,
No dewy tear nor downward look
As makeshift graves spread underfoot.

A vigil kept in greying light
Unmoved by those in soaring flight,
Nor tremble from her head held high
As preying winds gave their first sigh.

What deep desire made her stay
As night consumed remaining day,
Where came her strength to stand alone
As thorny air pierced skin and bone.

I watched till candlelight was spent
And ember red its warming glint,
Till sleep concealed from questioning eye
Her lone silhouette upon night sky.

Ice white dawn, fleeing mist
Light touching dark with fingertips,
A lone lament from bird on high
A mantra sad, a last goodbye.

My pure white rose in still of night
Closed her heart to winter's rite,
On her glittering shroud lay berries red
Death's tribute on a rime swathed bed.

STORY V

Cobblestone Streets

Long before delivery vans and lorries were seen on the roads, most deliveries and collections of goods were done by *Carters*. The word Carter is of Irish, Scottish and English origin and is an occupational name given to one who transports goods by cart or wagon. The name is originally believed to be of Gaelic and Celtic origins.

My father was a Carter; his daily companion was a very large Clydesdale horse named Tom.

If Tom could have talked, I'm sure he would have told me a story, much like one I have penned here…

Cobblestone Streets

I stood in a mist of steamy breath, overnight the temperature had dropped to zero turning my sleeping quarters into a makeshift Turkish bath. I moved around impatiently. In the quietness of the early morning the town clock struck five muffled strikes, soon my working day would begin. Minutes later a key turned in the lock of the heavy wooden door, it rattled loudly as the iron bar was withdrawn with a thudding clang. The master came in puffing and blowing. In the dim light of his lantern he looked like an overgrown bear, his thick black cape hung almost to the ground, warm gloves and thick muffler completed the picture. "Good morning Tom," he shouted light-heartedly. How I loved this man. "It's a raw morning," he continued talking as he placed my breakfast before me.

Half an hour later we were on our way, moving with a noisy clatter along the dimly-lit cobblestone streets. On summer mornings, the master sang and whistled, I really enjoyed all the songs and tunes, but on mornings like these there was very little talk, let alone singing, from the silent figure crouched on the seat of the cart.

Down at the railway station I met up with some of my friends. The impatient stamping of hooves on the icy ground echoed around the station yard like rolling thunder, the train was late, or else my friends were early.

All the carters were wrapped up warmly and stood in a huddle around a brazier of glowing coke, an occasional loud laugh escaped from the middle of the sea of capes. The capes parted as my master and I approached, I watched as a welcoming mug of steaming tea was reached into his gloved hand.

An hour later the train puffed and shunted its way from the yard and into the station to pick up early morning passengers. Our cart, like the other carts, were piled high with a variety of goods in all shapes and sizes, "a heavy one today Tom", the master sounded almost sorry as he pulled on the reins and guided me and the cart through the yard gates.

It was mid-afternoon by the time we had finished delivering our load to all the different warehouses around the town. My tired shoulders and pangs of hunger told me we were almost at the end of another working day.

As soon as we entered the stables the master removed my harness and collar, I gave a shudder, the sweat under them, which had been warm, now turned cold. "Just a minute big man," the master spoke as he struggled to remove his cape and muffler. I knew that instead of seeing to his own needs he would rub me down with a coarse cloth. He worked quickly, and minutes later I felt my body begin to warm. I neighed softly. He patted my head knowingly as he placed a good-sized barrel of oats in front of me.

After my meal I turned to Ben, the occupier of the next stall and the youngster of our group. Poor Ben, he was almost asleep on his feet. I didn't disturb him, I knew all about the bone-weary tiredness that comes in the first months of carting, I also knew that given time, Ben would get used to it and become like me…just tired. The master lifted his old leather bag, a signal that said the rest of the day and night belonged to me. "See you in the morning Tom" he shouted, as he disappeared through the door. I shook my head in reply and in the knowledge that I've had a good life and a kind man to share my days with. Soon both of us will retire, the master to the country cottage he always talks about, and me to the fields and stable that comes with it, both of us have had enough years of town life, cobblestones and early mornings.

Minutes after the stable door was locked and bolted, I closed my eyes, seconds later I was casually strolling across a dew-wet field, the scent of summer flowers drifted to my nose and a soft morning breeze rippled through my mane…

I stayed contently in the field until I heard, "Good morning Tom". Another working day was about to begin, but I didn't complain, for the master and me, it was another day nearer to green pastures…

The Little Lost Lamb…

At one stage in my life, three of my children were all in their adolescent years, seventeen, sixteen and fifteen respectfully. The teenagers listened to my advice and then went and did their own thing. A mindset that used to have me doing a weekly count of the ever-increasing grey hairs! This chapter of life is a bit like a caterpillar changing into a butterfly, the difference being it only takes about two weeks for the butterfly to appear. Waiting for the emergence of my teenagers into adults, according to friends, might take years!

My one and only daughter had been dressed from birth, in pink with frills. As the years passed I still had a say in her dress code, without arguments. I put dress codes out of my mind until one night my daughter came downstairs, she would have passed for Miss Sally in the children's show, *Worzel Gummidge*! I was, as they say, flummoxed! I giggled and quickly turned away from my husband's wide-open eyes!

Music was another mystery, the vocals were either too loud or mumbled; worse still was the fact that all three favoured a different group or singer!

The teenage years came and went leaving football and dress codes behind. In their place, came the years of motorbikes, cars and boyfriends. Gone were the bright red cheeks and the many heated arguments. Now, we had grease, oil and endless cups of tea, for the stream of *just friends* as my daughter called any young man who would sit, pimply-faced in our front room!

Many parents could relate a different story in regard to their children's teenage years. Stories of how their beloved children got drawn into the world of drink and drugs. Many of these teens were, or had been, in higher education, and many were on the point of realising the dream they and their parents had worked so hard to achieve.

Being bullied and blackmailed in school can lead young people to look for a form of escape. Many times the escape is drink and drugs. A hidden lifestyle outside the home, when discovered, can bring conflict into the lives of parents and family members. Help is there, but sadly for many young people, the help comes too late. Please, remember in prayer, all people, regardless of age, who have a drug addiction.

The Little Lost Lamb...

The little lamb had wandered away
Away from the shepherd so kind,
Wandered away to the places
Where everything looked so fine…

As he travelled along the wide road
 He found pleasures so sweet and rare,
The broad road was so pleasant
 He decided to linger there…

Some other sheep were feeding
They had freedom to roam near or far,
So, he followed the road they were taking
Never thinking he'd drifted so far…

Not a thought did he give to his master
Who searched long and hard for his sheep,
Not a thought did he give to the anguish,
Nor the sighs of those who did weep…

The road led far from the sheep fold
His master, his staff and his rod,
It led to by-ways covered in briers,
Many dangers he passed on that road…

Then, one day he got caught in a thicket
He cried, "Kind shepherd please come
I can't move backwards or forwards,
I've tried till my body is numb…"

Cold and alone he lay there
Caught in the thorns that enfold,
No one heard his cries in the darkness
He knew he was far from the fold…

Then through the pain, a voice came to his ears
"Little lamb it's me, don't cry, don't fear
You wandered away from my loving care,
I'll soon have you home, I'll carry you there…"

As the lamb felt strong arms around him
His little heart so filled with love,
Love for a dear kind master… a master,
Who understands when lambs leave the fold…

The little lamb now was sleeping
Sheltered from harm and from cold,
The shepherd smiled as he carried him gently
His lost lamb… was back in his fold…

STORY VI

Ripples In a Fountain

I sat gazing at him like a lovesick teenager who had just experienced her first kiss. I blushed as sweet memories of this past summer crept into my mind. Memories of sunsets, breaking dawns and the glory we both shared in those magical hours.

We enjoyed a special relationship, one that took us beyond ordinary life that most people take for granted. A liaison that started with our first meeting, a bonding that unknown to us, would seal our destiny. Memory upon memory competed with each other, each one begging to be recalled.

Once more I felt myself drift into the velvet night hours where we shared our thoughts and dreams, hours spent by the riverside or on a deserted beach, times when we escaped the pull of gravity and walked among the planets.

I heard the audience's loud applause. I looked around hoping no one had noticed my momentary lack of attention. I studied the faces of the people gathered in the auditorium - old, young, wrinkled, smooth - all applauding and showing their appreciation for the man beside me. I felt I would burst with pride.

The clapping grew louder until it seemed to rise from the body of the hall like the thunder of a hundred horses' hooves. Suddenly the podium began to shake. I wakened with a start. Realisation hit me a few seconds later. I had been dreaming. I felt angry. I was angry. I had every right to be annoyed. Minutes later the disappointment evaporated and was replaced with the stabbing pain of loss.

Why did I still dream about the old days and him? I felt sad when

I thought of the empty days, months and years that lay ahead. Last week I had fooled myself into believing that it was time I retired. I liked the word 'retired.' It sounded nicer that the word 'redundant' - as a matter of fact anything sounded nicer than the real truth.

I had hidden behind words and titles for almost a week and now, like it or not, I had to come to terms with the awfulness of being literally dumped for a younger model. I had two choices - acceptance or fight back. I chose the latter.

After much deliberation I came up with the perfect plan. I felt a warm glow spread over me but then realised the heat came from the sun shining in the window. I turned quickly and was almost blinded by a shaft of sunlight. Then from the midst of the swirling golden rays, came the voice that had brought me so much heartache.

"Come on old faithful." I felt joy and anger rise within me. His choice of words would have been more suitable for a sheepdog that lagged behind after a day's work! And how dare he speak to me in that tone of voice as if nothing had happened. I tried to move away from his outstretched hand but he was quicker than me. I felt his touch, and as the saying goes *'everything else is history.'*

Both of us had been through a trying experience and were all the richer for it. He spoke briefly of his infatuation and how, on more than one occasion, he had been let down by that certain someone's whims and moods, not to mention her desire to be always in the press photographs.

Our separation has taught him that bright young things are not always as reliable as they are made out to be. As for me, I'll ensure that no new-fangled ideas will ever come within handing distance of him again.

I must end this entry.

Dear Diary, it is almost time for me to be picked up, but then that's as it should be when one shares their life with a university lecturer. I'm always on the go and as I have often related to you, my vagabond lifestyle does have its compensations, after all, not everyone can travel the world, doing what they love best and with a man they admire and respect.

What more could anyone ask, especially someone like me, who in today's age of technology is looked upon as an ancient of ancients - or to put it more kindly - an old-fashioned fountain-pen!!

The Quiet man...

Learning to drive and passing the test are the first steps to becoming a driver. To be a *good* driver means studying and putting into practise everything in the Highway Code and using common sense.

Knowing everything instantly is a no no for new drivers; for all Christians the same tenet applies. We need to make time to study the Bible, God's Highway Code and put into practice what we read. Daily life and the Christian life should run parallel with each other, but sometimes they don't. The new and not-so-new Christian can get distracted by the busyness of being… a breadwinner, housewife, teenager or a member of their chosen church family.

Fear, anxiety and much more can overtake our thoughts. As in the driving test, we need to do an emergency stop and talk to our Instructor… An Instructor who sometimes has been forgotten in our busyness.

God waits for us to turn to Him, to talk to Him, to worship and love Him, the way He loves us in our happy or sad times. Our God doesn't keep an appointment book and He doesn't mind what time of day or night we call on Him in prayer.

I may have passed the driving test but I was still a learner for countless months afterwards. As a Christian of many, many years I am still learning. God is my instructor and the Bible is my Highway Code. Both are my constant companions…

{I passed my driving test in 1970. The poem `The Quiet Man` is the account of that memorable day...}

The Quiet Man...

I sat in the white car, my face the same colour
And wondered again, is this worth the bother?
I watched lorries and cars dodge here and dodge there
Just like the bumper cars, at the annual May fair.

The man sat beside me, a man of few words
No greeting was uttered just, "You can proceed forward,"
Now, I wasn't used to this silence, I wanted to say
'Don't you think it's a beautiful sunshiny day?'

The man sat in silence with a so solemn face
What was he thinking?
Why did he not look, why couldn't he see
The beautiful gardens and the greenest of trees.

Suddenly, a motorbike came flying like a great buzzing bee
It seemed to be making a beeline, for little old me,
I stood on the brakes, what a noise I could hear
As I halted I thought, 'the angels seem very near.'

I looked at the man, his red face matched mine
When he spoke his voice was more of a croak,
He said, "I was going to ask you to do a quick stop
I'm glad you're a mind-reader and could read all my thoughts."

I set off again and went this way and that
Up steepest hills and down roads that were flat,
The man spoke again, "pull over there"
'That's good' I thought, 'now we can have a nice cosy chat.'

But, I was questioned on that Highway Code, and
I knew the answers were there, somewhere in my head,
The man sat like an owl, humming under his breath
As I fumbled the answers and nearly sweltered to death!

When he started writing, I closed my eyes tight
Wondering, did I pass, did I do everything right?
Those few minutes seemed to turn into years
My eyes were begging to let go of the tears.

Well I passed my test…
What a relief no one knows,
Except for the man, who waited
As I uncrossed my fingers and even my toes!

I thanked the man of few words and waved him goodbye
I'm sure I heard him give a small sigh,
That quiet man looked so worried to me
Perhaps, he had a pain where I couldn't see.

As I removed the L plates and stuck up the R
I realised, this is the first time I'm alone in the car,
Now I was a driver I wanted to roam
Then, I remembered my family… waiting at home.

You see I'm just a mother whose life is humdrum
But at heart I'm a young girl who loves to have fun,
And someday I'll get in my car and drive off on my own
That is, when my children are married and from the nest flown.

Then the thought came again, I'm all on my own…
Where, oh where did that quiet man go?
I'll find him and ask, "Please, would you drive me home
For things looked so different, the controls so bizarre
When I changed my L plate… to a brand-new R…"

STORY VII

Strange Bedfellows

I opened one eye and blew through my nostrils like an angry bull.

"Women," I muttered through clenched teeth. She stopped humming, then with her nose high in the air she turned and stared straight into my face. Seconds later she resumed her tune, and to my annoyance raised the pitch another octave.

"Women," I silently seethed. Why do they do it? All of them are the same. Just because they have to be up and about in the morning, they think no one else should sleep. Don't they realise an extra hour is appreciated, especially when a fellow has a busy day ahead.

I turned my back on the bane of my life and snuggled lower into my bed. Ten minutes later I was on the floor, all ideas of sleep gone. I stole another sneaky look at the *singer*. There she sat, as unconcerned as the flowers in May, giving herself a manicure and trying to look presentable.

She seemed to be in a world of her own and couldn't care less about me, and my much-needed sleep. Now if I'd been to an all-night party, I'd have crept in quietly and disturbed no one, not like her, making as much noise as the dustmen do each Saturday morning.

She turned around and looked at me. I pretended to be busy, all the while watching her with letterbox eyes. Slowly she drank her morning milk, and then climbed into bed. I knew that five minutes from now she would be sound asleep and I would be left sitting bleary-eyed.

Being wide-awake I decided to take a stroll in the garden. At this early hour it would be peaceful. I was wrong. The trees were alive with squawking birds. I watched their frenzied flight as they carried breakfast for their young. The poor old fathers were just like me - they didn't get a lie in either.

I returned to the house feeling rather disgruntled and crawled into bed, hoping I could fall back to sleep. After counting the proverbial sheep and reaching number twenty I gave up. All I could do to pass the time was chew my nails.

Then an itch started - right in the middle of my back, at a spot where I couldn't reach!

"What a way to start the day!" I grumbled, rubbing the itchy spot against the edge of the bed.

I was feeling really hard done by when I heard the back door open. It was Annabelle, the housekeeper.

"Morning Basil. I suppose she was late home, or should I say early. Did she wake you from a nice sleep?"

I began to feel a bit better at the sound of her caring voice, but it belonged to another typical woman always asking questions but never waiting for an answer. I sat on listening and kept my mouth shut.

"You poor old thing," she continued with her one-sided conversation. Then like a magician, in-between talking and giving me a big hug, she produced my breakfast.

"Women," I mused, in between mouthfuls. 'We can't live with them and we can't live without them, especially at meal times!"

Women, I often stress, are a species apart from any other on earth and almost any right-thinking man finds them too complicated to try and understand. As for early morning adolescent females, what more can I say? I suppose we all have to tolerate some things in life.

Looking back, perhaps there's a slim chance that I disturbed people when I was young. I went back to my bed. I knew Petunia (what a ridiculous name!) would be there, snoring.

They say that actions speak louder than words. I agree, but creeping into my bed without as much as saying sorry is a bit much. I stood for a few minutes looking down on the nuisance. She was very attractive - no wonder she was invited to late night parties and get-togethers. I slipped into bed beside her. It was really hard not to love her, even with her faults. I bent over and nuzzled her ear. She opened and closed one eye, gave a contented sigh and snuggled closer.

I don't tell my friends about my home life, sleeping quarters, or Petunia the cat. If I did, they would laugh and think I was the silliest Alsatian in town. In the end though, does it really matter what others say? After all, a friend is a friend, regardless of size or gender…

STORY VIII

Urban Nights...

I sensed the midnight hour from my built-in clock. I stretched and yawned, then after a few wake-up shakes I went into the kitchen, all the while musing to myself about the silly dreams I had had in the last few hours. Suddenly breaking into my thoughts, it came, the scratching. I froze, then on tiptoe I edged myself towards the door and listened. "Well of all the cheek" I muttered through clenched teeth, "it's that scoundrel I chased last week." I breathed deeply as I backed away from the door, "right I'll show him a thing or two." I seethed in silent anticipation as I prepared myself to charge like a war-horse on the unsuspecting pest.

"Lucky so and so…" I said, remembering the rule of no swear words within earshot of the household. The air around me should have been bright blue as I climbed out from a pile of soggy newspapers, cabbage leaves and potato peelings, items that should have been put in the bin and not outside the backdoor! In frustration, I picked the last peelings from my hair. I was so glad the rest of the family were sleeping and didn't have to witness my humiliation.

I still had a whiff of tonight's dinner about me as I sat on the garden wall, it was an ideal place to view my friends' garden, not to mention the fact that this was the only place where I had peace to reflect on the world at large. I had just settled myself when a car roared up the road, "poor guy", I thought sarcastically, "he would be docked before he reached the roundabout!" The driver had to be a stranger, all the locals knew that the police wagon hides at the bend in the road! I really was in a foul mood. I decided to take a good long walk to clear my head.

I wandered slowly towards the Refuse Collection Centre, or as I call it 'the dump', I wondered if men in high places could find nothing better to do, other than decide on fancy names for a place that is simply used for throwing things away. I decided there and then to find out if any of my friends were on good terms with the council, how I would love half an hour in one of those swanky offices. I would be delighted to leave them a few suggestions in their suggestion box!

I reached my destination in time to witness a noisy, badly organized fight. Blood was flowing from the nose and ears of both opponents. I veered off to the right. I preferred my face the way it was!

A few minutes later I stopped dead in my tracks, the sound of shuffling feet came to my ears, my heart started to pound as the shuffling grew louder. I was ready to hightail it out of there when who should come strolling out from behind a pile of cardboard boxes, none other but *himself*, my Irish friend who lived two doors down from our house. I gave a sigh of relief. *Himself* was the most laid-back character I ever had the good fortune to meet.

He nodded, I nodded back. At times he is a bit of *a know it all*, but we had agreed a long time ago to agree.

Himself decided, as he had nothing better planned, to join me on my late-night stroll. Carefully we picked our way through a lot of uninteresting items, a gaily-dressed doll caught my eye, which on closer inspection had no arms, a jar of rusty screws with the lid screwed on tight, the usual collection of odd socks and an ancient washing machine! My thoughts turned again to the hierarchy and the fancy name they tagged this place. If they would just spend a few minutes here, instead of drinking coffee and eating cream buns, they would see that this place was in plain and simple terms just '*the dump*'.

We were about to take the road back home when we both saw her at the same time. In the moonlight her long hair sparkled like diamonds, she was the most beautiful foreigner we had ever seen. We thought her to be Asian, *Himself* looked at me and gave a wink, I winked back! "An introduction is called for" he said, his eyes twinkling. I simply agreed!

At that moment, who should swagger on to the scene, none other than one of the blood-stained fighters. What happened next made our mouths' fall wide open in surprise. The fighter limped up to this picture of beauty and she began wiping his blood-covered ear; from the smirk on his face we supposed she was also whispering sweet nothings into it! Turning our backs on the sickly love scene and feeling well and truly miffed, we decided this time to make our way home.

The town hall clock rattled out six strikes as we entered our street. "Will I see you tomorrow night Sam?" *Himself* asked between yawns. I nodded my head, still thinking about the date that might have been.

I left my friend dallying up his driveway and took a shortcut to my own front door. I'm a keep-fit addict and I didn't see any sense in walking past three enormous gardens when it was so easy to jump the walls between the houses!

Half an hour later I was settled in bed. As my eyes closed I decided to forget about the council twits, pimpernel mice and beautiful foreigners. My friends know I am not the type that holds grudges or is jealous. Tomorrow night I will make sure my whiskers and tail are spotless… potato peelings, cabbage and soggy newspapers are a definite no, no!!!!

Countdown...

Anger, like love, is intrinsic; it is part of our make-up and has its place with all our other feelings. I remember one man who showed his anger almost on a daily basis. That man was our Maths teacher at the Secondary school.

The first time I met the red-haired teacher, I was eleven years old and in the company of thirty noisy equals. As we piled into his classroom, he eyed us up and down; then lifted a long ruler and the blackboard pointer. "These," he said; "have other uses." Silence descended; no further explanation was needed, we all got his message!

At the end of the lesson we walked quietly from the classroom. Crossing the yard to go to the Art class, some of the boys remarked; "He's a tough nut!" Those words would become obvious in the following weeks and years. Red knuckles, sore palms and sometimes a sore head, were the other uses accredited to the teaching aids.

By the second term the *tough nut* raised the level. One day, with arms flailing and face tomato-red, he did his interpretation of a war-dance; then fired the hard blackboard duster across the room, missing the window by inches! His show of anger was triggered by his three times explanation on how to calculate the circumference of triangles and rectangles! Of all his many missiles, books, chalk and ping-pong balls, his boiling rage and the blackboard duster left us in terror.

On our last day at school as each of us shook his hand, he couldn't hide the smile that accompanied his shaky voice, as he said; "No grudges..."

Many, many years later, our red-headed, hot-headed maths teacher became Principle of the school. I dread to think what he may have thrown at the unsuspecting teachers, if they stepped out of line!

Anger, what do you compare it with? I liken it to a volcano, before, during and after an eruption. A volcano is a quiet mountain, until nature upsets it; the same can be said of our anger. It can simmer for days before it reaches boiling point. Like a wakened volcano that spews its contents over everything in its path, our anger once unleashed, brings pain and hurt. However, there is a big difference, unlike a volcano we can feel remorse and try to repair the damage.

After the release of our pent-up anger there is reflective quietness, after a volcano erupts there is just quietness.

Countdown...

I stand in sweet tranquillity
Cloud bathed in my serenity,
A masquerade that blinds the eye
To churning anger drawing nigh...

With grumbling pain as in birth
Loud bellows echo from my girth,
In boiling river deep below
My fiery innards rage and glow...

From my blood-red flaming mouth
In turmoil I spit and shout,
From swollen belly I expound
And vomit contents on the ground...

With unleashed fury running free
I swallow those that cannot flee,
Clearing courtyards once again
Of mortal gifts from mortal men...

I stand amid the nakedness
Anger subdued within my breast,
Distant, proud, alone and free
Untouched by all humanity...

In loneliness I drift to sleep
In solitude no company seek,
My torment quelled, I leave behind
Scar on scar, since start of time…

This man...

Forty or more years ago, a well-paid job would normally have been offered to a person with a grammar school education. The company or business usually asked the applicant to forward two references. This was stress-free if your parents were influential with other influential people. The ordinary run-of-the-mill candidates had few choices of people they could approach. Nine times out of ten, the request would be made to their doctor, church minister or pastor.

I remember a church service about forty years ago. I was in the company of an acquaintance, he was not a regular attender, but he did appear some Sunday nights. As we entered the vestibule, his talk was about the prospects of a new job, and he hoped the Rector would give him a reference. He explained his choice was simple, other professionals were always busy and would ask a fee. I said nothing, but wondered where he had got the impression that preachers only worked on a Sunday!

I slipped into a pew and was surprised when my friend joined me. As the service progressed, I glanced at him, his eyes were closed. I wondered if he was asleep or just resting his eyes. I never found out until a few weeks later. The address that night covered the life of Jesus, it was a hard-hitting half hour for anyone who was not a Christian. As the service ended I glanced again at my friend, he was wiping his eye.

It was three weeks before I was able to attend church again. My acquaintance was already sitting in a pew and I joined him. I whispered; "What about your job prospects?"

"I got it!" He said, with a smile.

"Did his reverence help you?" I asked.

"No," he said, "I didn't ask." My friend knew by my face that I wanted to know more, he continued; "That Sunday night, I met Jesus and I took Him with me." He was smiling as he continued, "I explained to the manager that I was a Christian and the only reference I had was Jesus." The manager gave me a start date, shook my hand and said; "Jesus is my reference too."

That night I walked home with a spring in my step, in the knowledge that we have a wonderful God, a God who listens and answers the prayers of humble people.

This Man...

I went to church that Sunday night
Keeping job thoughts in my sight,
A reference was my chief aim
I hoped the preacher knew my name…

"What is this man to you?"
I heard the preacher ask,
"The gift he offers do you accept?"
The church was warm, I slept…

Then I heard a mother scold
"Why did you leave, why did you go?"
I listened as the child explained
"It was my Father's work; I must train…"

I sat with crowds upon a hill
Sharing food, eating my fill,
I saw this man heal sick and lame
Bless little children each by name…

As I spread branches on the ground
Singing came, the sweetest sound,
I heard the people all proclaim
"This is He, our own true King…"

I stood inside Gethsemane's gate
I saw the kiss that sealed his fate,
His eyes conveyed to closest friends
It now begins, soon it will end…

I heard angry words in Pilate's hall
The words of Peter filled with gall,
"This man
This man… I don't know at all…"

In a prison cell I turned away
As whip and lash had their say,
Then Pilates rage, "take Him away
I find no guilt in Him this day…"

The scene then changed to Calvary
I stood beside the rough-cut tree,
I saw His blood, His wounded limbs
Then darkness fell and covered Him…

"This man, what is this man to you?"
It was the preacher's voice, I was in my pew,
"Was he just a man…
Just a man from the book I've read…"

"This man, the gift he offers do you accept?"
I was awake,
I lowered my head, the church was warm
I closed my eyes… I wept…

STORY IX

Contentment

Old Nell ambled her way along the crowded street. Every so often she stopped to admire the variety of goods in the shop windows. It was one of her favourite pastimes. Another was going to see weddings.

She had just spied a pretty blue cushion in Mr Taylor's shop window when she heard a peal of bells. From experience, she knew she'd have to hurry. In the last eight years she had been to see most weddings in the village church. It had become a habit, and habits of course were hard to break.

Slightly out of breath, but still with a few minutes to spare, she reached the church. Well-wishers were already there, patiently waiting for the happy couple to appear. Nell looked round, spotting the trail of rose petals.

"Perfect, just perfect," she said, as she walked along the edge of the beautiful perfumed bridal path.

Seconds later, the church door opened. With a little push and a few nudges, she managed to struggle through the crowd. Without showing any embarrassment, she climbed the two steps to the church door and stood beside the bride.

The happy couple just had time to smile and thank her for coming when all three were suddenly surrounded by guests throwing confetti. Nell lingered a few more minutes, then quietly slipped away. She really didn't like all the hustle and bustle.

Less than half an hour later she was strolling through the hayfield. She felt happy and content with her life as she walked along, watching the sun dancing through the trees.

The hayfield was soon forgotten as into view came a partly-ploughed field. Then the voice of a farmer came to Nell's ears. "Easy boy, easy." She watched as the red-faced man struggled to keep in step with the enormous plough horse, unconcerned, it plodded happily along with the bells on its collar jingling.

At the edge of the hayfield she followed the winding path along the river. She stopped to watch a family of swans, but moved on quickly when one of them started to climb the bank.

Without looking back, Nell made her way along the riverbank until she reached the old iron turnstile beside the small stone bridge. She rested for another few minutes, then crossed the road and into the lane that led to Jane's house.

Ten minutes later she arrived at the bright red door. It was open. Although Jane was not in the kitchen, Nell knew she was expected.

Settling herself on one of the comfy armchairs to wait for her friend, she looked around the kitchen she loved. It was homely and peaceful, and always filled with lovely cooking smells. She felt her eyes closing as she listened to the low steady tick of the grandfather clock. The armchair was just too comfortable.

Nell dozed for about half an hour, only wakening when she heard the clink of tea- cups. Jane was busy at the table.

"Come on old sleepy head," her friend said teasingly. Nell moved from the chair towards the table. She watched in anticipation as the contents of a large jug were poured carefully into a dish. Delicious is the best and only word she could think of to describe Mary's home-made custard that was made with milk straight from the cow.

Mary chatted non-stop for about ten minutes; then offered Nell some buttermilk, another home-made delicacy.

Half an hour later when the dishes were washed and put away, Mary settled down with her knitting. Nell sat with her eyes closed and listened to the click-clicking of the needles. She felt so happy and contented with her life. After all, what more could an old black cat ask for, than good friends, a cosy arm-chair and a great big bowl of sweet warm milky custard!

Heavenly light...

When my children were small and just days after the last fairy-light had been packed away, I started saving for Christmas the following year. I wonder how many of you reading this did the same.

Even in the '60s, it was so easy to get caught up in the materialistic madness of shopping and buying presents, then and more so now, the birth of Christ has been misplaced amid wrapping paper and string. If we all could take a few minutes and stand at the stable door, the fairy lights and shiny treetop star would grow dim in the light that shines from the crib.

The sleepy town of Bethlehem didn't see the dark stable set aglow in the light of the guiding star, the shepherds with their lanterns, the wise men in their fine robes and the light emitted by the heavenly angels. They didn't see God's light as it shone on His Son, the Christ Child. A child that one day would guide and lead men from darkness to the glorious light of salvation.

Heavenly Light...

Tucked up in bed with red rosy cheeks
My children lay in peaceful sleep,
It was Christmas Eve; it was late at night
And the tinsel star on the tree shone bright.

My home was cosy that winter night
Cosy and warm with curtains closed tight,
As I sat dozing by the warm log fire,
My thoughts drifted to a humble byre.

A noise made me turn to my colourful tree
Somehow, the star had fallen free,
As I placed it again on the topmost branch.
The curtain got caught on the window sash.

From the chink in the curtain, I saw starlight
Stars that glimmered in the dark of night,
Silver lanterns shining so bright
Keeping watch over earth, this Christmas Eve night.

Standing there, I thought again
Of the little town called Bethlehem,
And how a star had guided all
To a baby sleeping in a manger stall.

Just then the church bell chimed
And Christmas Eve was left behind,
As I listened again to the church bells ring
I looked at the tree and man-made things.

My tinsel star once bright, now dimmed
As the light of the Christ Child entered in…

STORY X

The Tears of God...

I penned this short story in memory of all the people who died, and for those who survived the Holocaust. In time the human body can be healed, but the spirit and soul is scarred forever with memories…

The man in my story could be *anyone* of these broken people… people who live with shadows…

The Tears of God...

The sky was dull and overcast as I made my way along the familiar path. Overhead the grey clouds kept the impending rain hidden. Ahead of me I could see and hear my friends, friends who accepted and trusted me without question. Most people who came to the park knew me on sight but there were some, especially strangers, who still made whispering remarks. I was more bemused than annoyed when I overheard their description of me. An eccentric, a curiosity, just an old misfit who comes to feed the birds, little did they know I'd been called worse.

Minutes later I stood in the middle of a large flock of pigeons. I love these greedy birds. I love their bright eyes and their friendliness. I love how they come so close and how they take flight freely at any given moment. I took a handful of crumbs and scattered them. Before they all fell to the ground, some were lifted in the breeze and swirled in mid-air. The sight brought back memories of snowflakes and bitter cold. Coldness that tittering strangers and this generation had never known. A coldness that penetrates the heart and soul. A coldness that devours the spirit and leaves an empty shell. Shells that are still searching for answers...

I dipped into the bag again and touched the soft crumbs. Brown and white crumbs mixed together, both crumbs, their colour telling of bleached and unbleached grain.

Once long ago I lay with others. All of us, like the breadcrumbs, labelled the same, no one noticed that we were each different. Young and old, family, friends and strangers, all of us mixed together until we had almost lost our identity.

All of us sharing the same putrid air. Rancid air that had been used and re-used a million times over, making each breath a labour, as the vomit crept from stomachs repulsed and hollow with hunger. In the darkness, our ears were filled with the unceasing moans and prayers of each other. Prayers to a God who had deserted us. A God who had turned away from us. What had we done? What was the awfulness we had committed?

I was just past my eighteenth birthday. A year that held the beginning of childhood dreams. Marta and I had always been sweethearts, we could have been married but decided to wait and finish university first. We knew that five years would be a long engagement, but what was five years in a lifetime of togetherness? We were happy. Our families were happy, and everything was perfect in our small world.

Then it happened. The madness. Like a creeping long-fingered shadow, it covered and swallowed us. In a blink of an eye all our dreams and hopes turned into a nightmare of despair.

A splash of rain on my face brought me back from the past. Hurriedly I sprinkled the remaining crumbs around me. The pigeons gobbled them up quickly. Memories crowded my mind again. I thought of the months spent begging and grovelling for a piece of stale bread, I thought of Marta, my mother and sisters. Did they die of hunger? Or did they go on a last train journey? I had no way of knowing. They were so near in thought, yet so far away. Beautiful Marta, I still see her scared eyes as they parted us at the gate. We had listened to the promises. We thought we would be together. I can still see her being pushed and prodded with the rest of the women. Scared, frightened, despairing, no words can describe the look on the women and children's faces. No words can describe the terror that awaited them. Why did I survive? What purpose did my deaf God have in allowing me to live?

I reached deeper into my bag and brought out the tightly wrapped package. The drizzling rain trickled into my eyes. I was thankful to feel the wetness. I couldn't cry. I had no tears. I opened the small parcel. Slowly I caressed the old chipped frame and then my eyes lovingly savoured each tiny piece of the brown tinged photograph. There in the palm of my hand, crossing the divide of years and pain came the smile. The smile I wanted to see again, the smile I wanted to trace with my finger.

The rain poured down. Some of my friends sheltered in the trees as others left on the wing. I turned and walked back along the familiar path towards the park gate. A few minutes later I had reached the main road. I stood quietly watching humanity pass by; then I joined them to walk the short distance to my lodging house. Some people glanced at me and smiled, others looked and turned away tittering. They had a right to titter at an old man. An old man, who walks through the heavy rain, with a large umbrella swinging on the crook of his arm. Perhaps I am a curiosity and an oddity in other people's eyes. If I am, so be it, it doesn't really matter. God knows who I am. He knows my heart. He knows that at times I am angry with Him and the world, yet I know He loves me.

I walked slowly, I was in no hurry to leave the refreshing rain that splashed on my face and trickled into my eyes. I am thankful for the wetness. I am at peace. The hurting is over for another day. I am stilled in my heart. The Tears of God rest gently upon my cheek…

Soul music...

From the moment we are born and into old age we are given titles. I was *'the baby of'*, *'the daughter of'*, *'the sister of'*, *'the aunt of'*, the *wife of'*, *'the mother of'*, *'the grandmother of'*... where was I? I used to get frustrated when I was introduced as anything except me! I seemed to disappear in strings of *'this is'*... As time passed I got used to being a *'this is'*, but there was still a part of me that wanted to be recognised by my Christian name.

It took umpteen years before that came to pass. Sixty to be precise! It was the day I graduated and the day my birth name of Elizabeth became public for the first time. I was pleased, here I was at long last recognised, I was no longer a *'this is.'* I was an *'I am!'* I had finally achieved my identity. In truth, I loved all the titles I had inherited over the years.

Some people lose their identity through no fault of their own. Bankruptcy, redundancy, retirement and various addictions, all these and more contribute to many people becoming none persons. Negative thoughts and loss of self-worth are crushing blows to someone who was once a part of society.

We can see these invisible people lying drunk on the footpath, or begging on a street corner. We see them with blind eyes.

God knows all His sheep and calls each of them by name.

Soul Music...

I almost passed him by that day
Against a crumbling wall he lay,
An old black dog shared his home
Two tattered coats on ageing bones.

A life forgotten now by life
As busy world rushed past with wife,
At pity pennies cast in haste
He raised his cap, I saw his face.

Then, from his pocket came a flute
A pipe of tin, scratched, bent and mute,
When held within his wrinkled hand
It seemed to change to magic wand.

As pipe was touched by fingers thin
Sad music came from deep within,
A ghostly air, a nameless tune
Refrains of love, despair and doom.

From a battered pipe aged and old
Came sounds that touched my inmost soul,
I stood within the sad embrace
I felt the pain, but not the grace.

The music swirled and curled around
Spinning over tree and ground,
Then rising as on eagle wing
It mingled with the clouds of spring.

The music kept with me that day
In restless sleep the flute still played,
Then, in dawning light came inward sight
And friendship's hand to man with pipe.

But my tomorrow came too late
The man of mystery couldn't wait,
He'd disappeared in sinking sand
Swallowed up by muddy land.

Regretful tears, my tears of shame
I knew his face but not his name,
A hurting man by an old stone wall
With a pipe of tin and a weeping soul…

Apathy…

Little did Wilbur and Orville Wright know in 1903 that their first flying machine would become one of the greatest inventions of the twentieth century.

The aeroplane has had many uses over the past one hundred years; the one I remember will stay with me always.

The aeroplane was used as a carrier of compassionate aid for the famine in Biafra. These journeys were named Mercy Flights. That is exactly what they were, empathy dropped in food parcels to the thousands of starving men, women and children. In many cases the food did not reach the people in time and sadly for countless unnamed people, there was no mercy.

I penned, **Apathy**, lest we forget. Hope… A warming fire… Despair… The discarded ash.

Apathy...

Deep empty pools endless wait
On life to fall from flying crate,
Mouthed screams and silent sighs
Upward rise to cloudless sky.

Wells of hope dry up and die
Birds of life have passed on by,
Unneeded now is hungers lust
As breath returns to first formed dust.

Covered with an earthen rug
Echoes stilled in sun-baked mud,
Spirit shadows stalk the land
The seeds of Adam, lie hand in hand.

Again...

I penned the poem '***Again***' in memory of all the innocent people that were killed or maimed in the Omagh bombing. This tragic incident was a car bombing that took place on 15th August 1998 in Omagh in County Tyrone Northern Ireland. It took the lives of 29 people and injured 220 others.

May we who are a part of this strife-torn land pray for all the devils' workmen, that they may see through new eyes the hurt and pain they inflict on their fellow-man.

Again...

The devil's workmen came that day
Along the market street they strayed,
Watching and waiting for the chance
To steal a life with death's sharp lance.

The devil's workmen, devious, lay
Choosing with care their easy prey,
Waiting for that moment in time
When bells would toll a mournful chime.

The devil's workmen chose that day
Their guarded game to put in play,
Success would show in grief and pain
To maim and mar was their chief aim.

The devil's workmen came that day
Shadows blighting sun's bright ray,
Leaving death trails on the way
Snatching innocents at play.

The devil's workmen heard the cries
But strolled away with laughing eyes,
Pockets filled with blood-stained pay
Their work complete… for another day…

No copyrights...

As a child, trying to copy a picture from a book was one of my favourite pastimes, I was thankful I had rubber-tipped pencils! As children, another type of copying was that of imitating some of the local shopkeepers. Our voices would become high-pitched like the greengrocer, or we would spend ages sniffing like the butcher, or stutter like the milkman! The shoemaker was another that had us almost choking, his voice was always muffled, due to a mouthful of tacks, and no, we didn't put tacks in our mouth, just pieces of cloth! One of our favourites was the rag man; some of the boys had his call of, *'any old rags, any old rags?'* down to a tee. I'm sure many of you played these silly childhood games.

In 1996 the game of copying took on a new dimension. That was the year Dolly the sheep was cloned. I and many people worldwide were devastated that man, in the interests of science was playing God. Scientists played the game of creating the physical body of an animal. The question arises, will man ever create man and will he try to copy the soul? Twenty plus years have passed since Dolly was born; science has travelled far in the quest for knowledge and power. Science needs to take a step back and think of how the universe came into being and who created it.

Do animals have souls? Do they go to heaven? These two questions bring heated debate, some believe, others not. I believe what I read in the Bible.

In Revelation, the Apostle John's vision of Heaven also included animals, showing Christ and the armies of Heaven riding on white horses (Revelation 19:14). The prophet Isaiah says God will include animals in the new heavens and a new earth, *'The wolf and the lamb will feed together, and the lion will eat straw like the ox, and dust will be the serpent's food. They will neither harm nor destroy on all my holy mountain, says the LORD.'* Isaiah 65:25.

We, who believe in creation, have no voice to stop the rapid pace of the scientific world. What we do have is a God who will speak and when He does, the whole universe will tremble.

No Copyrights...

Perfection graced the hallowed ground
No shadow cast, nor echo sound,
In swirling mist it came to bless
An imaged self that lay at rest...

Revealed at last the master plan
Pleasure of the Spirits' Hand,
Brought forth from a patent source
A mirrored form of all life force...

Innocence, blinded by evil's sting
Parleyed with choice, as death bells ring,
Shadows form in unblemished light
Covering shame in perfection's sight...

Since time was and life began
Darkness strived for the soul of man,
Complete dominion its one last role
Infinite copyrights of a mirrored soul...

Perfection's template in endless time
Perceives the dark misguided mind,
As imaged man strives to imitate
The template speaks ... eradicate...

STORY XI

Backward Glances

Chapter one
Trunks and secrets...

"What a load of old rubbish!" I said loudly. Anyone listening to me would also have picked up on my annoyance. I was trying to manoeuvre myself between a two-legged piano stool and five deck chairs; at the same time dodge the umpteen spiders that hung like trapeze artists from the ceiling and light fitting. Either they were dead, mummified or scared stiff, but for whatever reason they never moved. I left them alone and studied the clutter in around of me.

The estate agent had insisted that I check everything and that was what I was doing. I had left the attic until last, knowing there was nothing in it I would want. I glanced at my watch. Another half-hour was all I needed and then I could turn the key for the last time on the family home and memories. I wondered where to begin. Finally, I decided to start in one corner, but not before opening the small window, allowing fresh air to enter and the stale mustiness to escape for the first time in years.

I lifted a few broken picture frames and empty boxes out of my way.

"Why would anyone collect empty boxes?" I muttered as I slowly pushed, pulled and slid everything from the corner. I sat down to catch my breath on a pouffe that had half its stuffing hanging out.

So far, out of all the clutter, all I was going to successfully bring home with me were laddered tights and broken fingernails! It was beginning to look like everything would end up in the dump. I lifted one of my old tattered teddy bears and was about to throw it out with the rest of the rubbish when I changed my mind. I turned to set it with my handbag when I spied the trunks almost hidden from sight behind an old chest of drawers in the opposite corner. My curiosity was aroused.

It took me longer than I thought it would to move everything around. The sweat was breaking on my brow, not to mention another broken fingernail and a cut on my ankle! When I did manage to haul the three trunks into the middle of the floor, I felt shattered. I sat looking at them. They were old and bound with leather straps. I never remembered seeing them when I was growing up. Perhaps my mother had picked them up at a jumble sale just before she became ill. I wondered what lay inside them. Forgetting my tiredness, I quickly unbuckled the straps.

"Oh Mother!" my overloud words were repeated again as I gazed in disbelief at the contents of the first trunk. It was crammed with old-fashioned, mothball smelling dresses and an assortment of hats and scarves. A note was neatly pinned to one of the faded musty shawls. In my mother's handwriting were the words, 'these belonged to my grandmother and her sister.'

"Oh Mother!" My voice was gentle this time. "Why did you keep these?" For a moment I imagined her laughing at my frustration; then I felt my eyes filling with tears when I remembered how much she loved me.

I had started to repack the trunk when I spotted the shiny beads peeping out from the torn lining on the inside of the lid. As I reached in to lift them, my hand brushed against a little book. *"What have we here?"* I wondered, as I pulled it out of its hiding place. The delicate cloth cover was almost paper-thin. I opened the book with great care and was surprised to see that although the pages were discoloured, the handwriting was readable. I glanced at my watch, the half hour I had intended to stay was now nearing an hour. I settled myself more comfortably on the pouffe and decided to read a few pages. Another ten minutes wouldn't make that much difference to my schedule.

Monday 20th August 1860...

Our new English tutor is most irritating. How can we, who have been born on England's small sister island, be expected to use the spoken word to perfection? We are Northern Irish and almost everyone in class, including myself, has a slightly different dialect, which, I must admit, to a newcomer can be confusing. In due time, Miss Harvey will understand our peculiar speech. I must pay more attention and persevere with nouns, verbs and all the intricacies she so patiently repeats at each lesson.

I took Bonny out for an after-supper canter. It was a beautiful evening and I had miles of uninterrupted pleasure by myself. I rode like the wind. If Papa had seen me, I would have been reprimanded most severely.

Tuesday 21st August 1860...

Today we had more lessons. Sometimes I feel this new science is getting quite beyond all sense of reason, yet I am compelled to peruse it with all eagerness. I do understand these lessons are new and not fully introduced into society. According to our mentor, one day, all classes and creeds, not just the educated will be able to interpret formulas and such.

Close friends of my elder sister remarked that this new science is primitive and boorish. I disagreed and did my best to explain my interest in all methods of measure and so on. I enjoyed my game of tennis this afternoon, but I fear I shall need more practice!

Wednesday 22nd August 1860...

After my refreshing canter across the downs this morning I spoke with Papa. He is an avid reader and always retreats to the quiet sanctuary of the library after breakfast. Dearest Papa, never happier than when he has his nose in a book. He is an extremely learned man, having travelled all over the world in his younger years. I enquired if he had any books on the different breeds of horses, to which he started to talk about the time he spent in Arabia.

Papa paints the most colourful pictures when he speaks about his expeditions. I had to interrupt him after an hour, as I was due to take luncheon with Mama and Aunt Matilda. No lesson tomorrow or Friday. Next Monday should be interesting. I have been invited to attend an oration entitled 'Formation of Schooling', at the Manor. Which reminds me, I must purchase some pretty handkerchiefs on Saturday. Goodnight little book, I shall be overly busy during the next few days, but I shall record little snippets on the evening of Monday.

I laid the almost disintegrated little journal carefully down on the faded carpet. Suddenly multi-coloured dust particles that had lain invisible for years between the pages appeared like shiny pearls, only to disappear again into the shafts of sunlight that danced in through the small attic window. For a moment I wondered about the dust and the day it had become trapped. The thought disappeared as I lifted the two brown-tinged photographs that had slipped unnoticed onto my lap.

One was of a fine Georgian house set in extensive grounds. On the back of the photo was the name Mr Samuel Blemmin. This second photo had me excited and fumbling for my glasses to get a better look. Three of the most handsome thoroughbred horses I had ever seen looked back at me from the brown-edged photo.

I had spent the last fifteen years breeding and showing my much-loved horses, and I knew the ones in the photograph were rare and almost priceless. I laid the photos beside the book and looked around again at the jumble of items that had been collected over more than two lifetimes. The three trunks held memorabilia of my late grandmother and her sister Emily. My grandmother and then my mother had kept them safe all these years. Now I had to decide whether to do the same or have a bonfire!

Before Mother died two months ago, she left the decision with me as to whether I would sell the family home or not, I knew my decision would not be hard to make. Yorkshire held nothing for me except happy childhood memories and the family grave. I had agreed just yesterday with the local Rector, a fixed sum to ensure the grave would be kept tidy. My inspection of the house was the last item on the agenda. I lifted the little book again and looked at the few faded entries. I knew very little about my late great aunt, except that I had been given her name. As for my grandmother, she was a very private person who seldom spoke about her family. As a child, I remember her as being a very gracious lady, who at times would brush my hair gently and say it reminded her of another head of auburn curls. I was about six years old when she died and I never remembered my grandfather; my own father had been killed in the Second World War and my mother never remarried. I was her only child and she spent the rest of her life living for me. I suppose I should have been thankful and agreed with the lifestyle she had planned for me, but I knew from an early age what I wanted to do. I remember her words the day I graduated: "Stubborn like your namesake."

Everything turned out fine in the end, although when mother did visit the farm she often remarked that a husband and family would be more in keeping than animals. Sometimes, just sometimes, I wish I had married, but Mr Right never did seem to appear on the scene, or perhaps I was too choosy. The years had flown and now I was only two months away from my thirty-fifth birthday. I consoled myself with the thought that some things are not meant to be, and long ago had accepted that the love and centre of my life were my horses.

I looked at my watch. Another hour had passed, but somehow, I didn't seem to mind. In reality I was glad of the opportunity to sit and think of the years between being a child and now. I blew my nose. '*Sentimental old fool*', I thought to myself as I reached down and gently lifted the little book back onto my knee. I started to read the delicate writing again. This time I read each sentence slowly instead of scanning the page.

My eyes picked up on the words, Northern Irish. They took me by surprise. Here I was, reading about a member of my family and not realising my bloodstock originated in Ireland. As I read on, I began to wonder if I had any distant relations a short plane journey away. My curiosity was aroused. I wondered who the whiskered gentleman by the name of Mr Samuel Blemmin was and what ever became of him. The attic room, although it reminded me of a junk shop, was warm and comfortable, but I felt the need of a cup of coffee, not to mention a breath of fresh air to clear my head - a head that was quickly filling with unanswerable questions.

Half an hour later I returned to the small room. This time I felt more at home with my surroundings and, forgetting about my expensive navy suit, I settled myself in an overgrown armchair. Question after question flitted into my mind. Why did my mother not tell me more of the family history? Perhaps she did and I was so busy doing my own thing that I took no notice. I settled back into the softness of the chair and closed my eyes, not with the aim of falling asleep, but to think. Slowly, little snatches of conversation started to come to my mind, childhood memories which had been of no use to me, that is, until now.

"You're Great Aunt Emily," my grandmother once said, "died just before she reached her eighteenth birthday." From the mists of memory came other words, telling of her horse rearing at a fence when she and a gentleman were attending the annual hunt. The fatal accident had proved too much for the family and they sold up and moved to Yorkshire.

My memories ended at that point. Why, oh why, did I never question family matters. Was my aunt buried in Ireland and not in the large family grave? Why had I never seen any pictures of her? Was it only my hair that reminded my grandmother of her? I felt the little knowledge I had gained over the last two hours was useless and decided to inspect the trunks thoroughly once more, just in case I had missed some little piece of information. Perhaps somewhere among all the items I had overlooked was a photograph of my namesake.

I searched through the musty-smelling trunks, but found no more photographs or anything that would connect with the little handwritten journal. Moth-eaten garments, feather boas and hair ornaments brought a smile to my face. For a moment, I began to understand why my mother had given all these useless family

Trunks and Secrets...

heirlooms houseroom. I also knew I would not be having a bonfire or sending anything to a jumble sale!

Slightly disappointed, I turned once more to the first trunk I had opened. I decided to tidy its contents and lock it up for its journey to Cornwall along with the other two. I knew the three old trunks would end up in my attic. Another smile came to my face as I pictured someone else opening them after I had departed this life.

I was bending over the trunk when my glasses slipped from my nose and disappeared between two moulting ostrich feathers and a sequinned jacket.

Everything had to be removed before I could reach in and lift out my glasses. It was then that my hand touched the small package, I felt rising excitement as I lifted it from the darkness and into the light. A faded green satin ribbon was tied around a linen type cloth. For a moment my mouth went dry. I knew this little package was special by its appearance and because it had been hidden. I felt a tinge of guilt as I carefully untied the ribbon, but my feelings did not deter me from finding out what lay concealed in secret. Slowly I revealed its contents. There, neatly folded, lay a yellowing lace trimmed hankie and two small envelopes, one dated 27th August 1860, and the other 30th December 1860. Without a second thought, I opened the first envelope, whose date and handwriting matched the last entry in the little journal. The small piece of faded notepaper had a ragged edge, as if it had been torn from the little book in haste. None but the writer was ever intended to read it. I pushed the feeling of guilt from my mind and read on.

Emily, 27th August 1860

When our hands met today in friendship, this pretty handkerchief slipped from my sleeve and brushed against his. I feel that a part of his spirit has been caught in the delicateness of the lace. I don't quite understand my feelings, but an unexplainable feeling tells me that a certain gentleman and I shall be in each other's company very soon. I dare not record these words in my book, so I shall conceal them forever and remember them often.

I felt like an intruder, yet I was compelled to open the second envelope. Again, the same faded notepaper met my eyes. The main difference was a break of four months between the two dates. This note, like the other one was private and for the writer's eyes only.

Emily, 30th December 1860

It is more than four months since I first met my dearest Samuel. How much we love each other. Seldom do we ever have the gift of being alone in each other's company.

Samuel is kept busy with the parish and his writings. It is much too soon for Samuel to ask Papa for my hand in marriage. We must be discreet for another three months until I reach my eighteenth birthday.

Our age difference will cause a few whispers and raised eyebrows, but what is twenty years when one is in love? Tomorrow night at the ball, he will hold me close and my heart will sing. My dream is to be his wife and to live with him near his family home in Portmoley. I have been there on one secret visit. How I loved the sea and the purple-topped mountains. I await springtime and my birthday with impatient longing. Samuel has promised me one of his fine horses as an engagement gift. I constantly dream of us both cantering across the fields with the wind rushing into our faces. I shall be counting the days until my dream becomes reality.

I sat holding the faded pages of notepaper for a long time. An overwhelming sadness filled me. Icy shivers ran down my spine as a cool breeze filtered in from the partially opened window. I was angry but also disappointed. Here I was in a dusty old attic and within the space of a few hours, had entered the life and times of a long-dead member of my family, someone who was just a name from my childhood, yet I could mentally build a picture of her from her writings. She was caring, strong-willed, inquisitive and had a love of horses.

My mental picture of Emily sounded as if I was describing myself, even down to my curly auburn hair! How I wished I had a proper photograph of her, of everything in the three trunks, the only photos I had were of the large house and the handsome horses. To say I wanted to know more is a slight understatement.

Who was Mr Samuel Blemmin? Did he marry someone else? Were any of his descendants still alive in Ireland? Did he keep account of his affair with Emily? He was an author, a man of words, perhaps somewhere, someone has answers to all my questions.

Another question filtered into my weary brain. Where was Emily buried, if the family moved to Yorkshire after her death? I knew in my heart that come what may, I had to find out.

I tidied up the attic and fastened the straps around the trunks. Into a small cardboard box I carefully placed the journal, package and photographs, almost reverently I carried it downstairs and placed it on the large kitchen table. I stared at the box and wondered what to do next.

Two cups of coffee later and I was back to my cheerful self. I spent the next half hour chatting over the phone to my farm manager. He assured me that everything was fine at home and things could run quite well without me for another few weeks. The second phone call lasted no more than a few minutes. My heart was thumping like a drum as I set the receiver down. I had booked myself on a flight to Ireland the following morning! I locked the door of my family home, knowing I could not make any decisions just yet in regard to its sale. I needed time to think and time to find out about two people who so long ago were very much in love.

Chapter two

An unexpected trip...

I settled myself in bed at 10pm. The hotel room was pleasant, but it was a far cry from my bedroom in Cornwall. My last thoughts before I went to sleep were of my much-loved horses and the horses in the faded photograph.

As I relaxed into my seat for the plane journey, I realised that at long last I had at least two hours to do nothing else except think. I put my Walkman earphones in, not to listen to music, but to cut myself off from the chatter and laughter of the other passengers. I closed my eyes and slowly thought once again about the events that had me winging my way across the Irish Sea.

"Complete and utter madness!" I knew I had spoken out loud the minute the words had formed in my head. Red faced and embarrassed, I slowly squinted around at my fellow travellers. From the continuing chatter it seemed no one had paid any attention to my outburst. If they did, they probably thought I had had a nip too much whisky! Removing the earphones, I lifted and drank the glass of liquid that sat in front of me. I smiled to myself as I called the steward and asked for another of the same - brown lemonade never tasted so good!

A few minutes before the plane landed, I casually glanced out the window. The sight that met my eyes made me gasp. Miniature trees and hedges in various shades of green, criss-crossed patchwork fields of gold and brown. The landscape reminded me of a home-made quilt - one that had been worked on for a long time with patience and loving care. For a moment I could almost imagine Emily cantering across those same fields, with the wind rushing through her hair.

"Fasten your safety belts please." The steward's voice interrupted my pleasant musings. Minutes from now I would be standing on the land of my ancestors, I felt as excited as Neil Armstrong did when he took his first steps on the moon!

I stood beside the conveyor belt, clasping my small overnight case with its precious contents and waited for the rest of my luggage. I was wondering what to do next when a pleasant-faced porter approached me.

"Do you need help?" he asked, lifting my bags from the belt and onto the floor. Within minutes this kindly man had guided me to the airport entrance; hailed a taxi and then informed the driver to take me to a good hotel.

I had been told that the Irish were friendly, now I was willing to believe it. Taxi drivers are the same the world over and this one was no exception. Before we had left the airport, he was chatting to me like a long-lost friend and by the time we reached the city, I felt I knew his wife and family personally. He in turn had gleaned enough rudiments on birthing a foal to running a farm in his spare time! Before leaving this talkative man, I asked if he knew of a place called 'Portmoly'. Unfortunately he didn't, but he suggested, along with umpteen other pieces of advice, that I try the Tourist Board. As I thanked him he gave me his firm's phone number.

"You might need my services again!" he shouted above the noise of the traffic. I smiled as he and his taxi disappeared down the busy road.

The hotel management and staff were helpful and friendly. The Tourist Board was not! I suppose my arriving ten minutes before closing was the reason. The best information they could offer was a list of government offices. I returned to the hotel armed with the list and a street map.

After dinner I studied the names of buildings and made a rough plan of where I would begin my search. Two hours later I fell exhausted into the soft bed. I was too tired to think any more. Slowly my eyelids and overworked mind couldn't resist the pull of sleep much longer, I reached out my hand and switched off the bedside lamp.

'Goodnight, Emily,' I whispered, as I pulled the duvet quilt over my head.

I was in high spirits as I set off on my quest the next morning. The sun was shining and everything seemed right with the world. By 3pm, my zeal and energy had been all used up. I was hot, hungry and tired, and it seemed I was on a wild goose chase. Of the many people I had spoken to, none could offer me any help. I had one more address left on my list but I didn't want to build up my hopes.

The old building resembled the many others I had entered since my search began that morning. A large brass plate with various departments inscribed on it told me I had reached my destination. Taking a deep breath, I entered the dark panelled hallway and knocked on the glass window with a 'reception' sign. I had grown weary three buildings ago, of being ushered from one department to another and explaining at least twice what I required. I had vowed from then on, that one explanation was sufficient. I was well rehearsed and ready for the pleasant-looking lady who appeared at the small window.

"May I speak with the manager?" I enquired in my most business-like voice. The look on the woman's face held many questions, but for whatever reason, she changed her mind and scurried off through a frosted glass door. I wondered if it was my accent, navy blue suit or briefcase, that did the trick. She was back almost instantly.

"Come this way please," she said, holding open the door. I thanked her and duly obeyed.

I entered a smoke-filled room. An ageing bespectacled man peered at me from behind an untidy, overly large desk, in the split second before he spoke, I felt his eyes travel from my feet to my tousled hair.

"Good afternoon and how can I be of service?" he asked in a lilting voice. I took the proffered chair and after introductions explained why I was in Ireland. Mr Thompson never interrupted my monologue. He sat listening, taking notes and nodding his head. When I had finished relating my story he simply said: "I see."

He then excused himself and left the room. I sat back in the comfortable well-scuffed leather chair, and let my eyes wander around the oak panelling and highly decorative plaster ceiling. Along one wall, three huge filing cabinets stood like untidy sentries, with buff coloured folders peeping out of their half-open drawers. Numerous papers and cardboard boxes seemed to live in every nook and cranny of the room. I wondered how anyone ever found anything among the clutter. The sound of the door opening and closing made me sit up. Mr Thompson had returned to the room.

"I believe we may be able to help you," he said smiling. My excitement must have shown on my face.

"But," he added quickly. "It will take time." I said I could wait; then felt foolish when he informed me that the office closed at 4pm. He did take time however to explain about the many searches he would have to carry out - birth, death and land certificates had to be found, not to mention old maps of almost one hundred years ago. Undeterred, I asked what time his office opened the following day. Mr Thompson smiled.

"I'll see you then at ten in the morning," he said, reaching over the littered desk to shake my hand. I left his musty old-fashioned office with wings on my heels. My hopes were at long last beginning to rise above ground level. The good feelings of this morning once again returned as soon as I stepped from the building and into the bright sunshine and bustle of city life. I had two hours to spare before I was due back at the hotel for dinner. So, like any other woman who finds herself in a large city with time on her hands, there was only one thing to do - go shopping!

At one-minute past ten the following morning, I entered the gloomy domain of Mr Thompson's office. He looked and said, "Good morning, you're keen."

His voice and face appeared through a cloud of tobacco smoke. Little did he know I was more than keen, I was desperate.

"Well now, Miss Blackburn," he continued. "You aroused my interest yesterday, so much so, that I took notes, files and such, home with me last night." I sat up straighter in the chair. "And?" My single word question hung in mid-air. Another puff of smoke drifted up to the ceiling before he spoke again.

"I have good and bad news. Which would you like first?"

Three hours later, I looked at the man sitting opposite me enjoying an overly large salad. He had insisted we both take time away from paperwork to eat. The small restaurant where he took lunch every day was cosy and intimate.

"Just the place to take our ease and talk at leisure," he said, over a small glass of sherry. Mr Thompson was a fatherly type of man and I knew he would give me the best advice possible.

My mind drifted back over what he had related to me that morning. Seemingly there had been a town-land called Portmoley, but it had changed name and owner many times, and all that remained on the land now was an old dilapidated graveyard that had not seen a burial for over fifty years.

The Blemmin family had been the landlords from 1600 to 1906 when they, for whatever reason, emigrated to Australia. As for my aunt, her name was on the original register as being baptised in the old church. Unfortunately the rest of the records had been lost when the church was destroyed by fire.

"More coffee?" Mr. Thompson's voice broke into my thoughts. We talked, or rather Mr Thompson talked about the West Coast and its remarkable beauty. I nodded in all the right places, but feelings of sadness filled me when I thought of the secret love that had only lasted for a brief time.

Back at the office we set about putting every piece of information into order. I wondered just how much midnight oil this considerate man had used. The afternoon seemed to slip past in a flash. We were only half way through the mountain of paperwork, when the receptionist entered and said it was time to close up shop, it was only then that I realised how tired I was.

"Can I come again in the morning?" I asked quickly.

"I took it for granted you would," Mr Thompson replied as he lifted his walking stick and briefcase.

I had mixed feelings that night as I went to bed. My head swam with questions. Should I visit the countryside that Emily loved, or should I go back home to Cornwall, the farm and my much-loved horses? In the darkness of the bedroom, the figures on the alarm clock glowed like beacons. It was almost 4am and I needed to get some sleep, so I did the proverbial thing and started to count sheep. I remember reaching five hundred and twenty-six. At that point I'll let the farmer count the rest!

The following morning I returned to the office. The receptionist took no notice of me as I walked past, except to say, "Good morning." She had remarked last night, in the nicest possible way, that I was becoming a part of the furniture. I settled myself on one side of the large desk with my dear kind friend opposite me.

Yesterday we sorted all the papers into a semblance of order, and this morning we were going to go through them with a fine-tooth comb. I made two lists of questions. I wanted to know if Samuel emigrated with the rest of the family or moved to another part of Ireland. What was the name of the ship? Where in Australia did it disembark? Samuel's list was growing longer and longer.

My questions concerning Emily were few. However, I knew that come what may, I would visit the townland where she grew up. I wanted to stand in her part of the world, even though it might be a built-up area. At least the ruins of where she had been baptised would still be around. I also wanted to see the purple-topped mountains that had been mentioned in her journal.

Mr Thompson seemed to take a long time to read my lists. I waited patiently for his comments. Would he understand my reasons for wanting to follow this through as far as possible? At last he spoke.

"Fine, Miss Blackburn and while you're away, I'll contact the shipping lines." I was at his side of the desk almost before he had finished the sentence.

"Thank you for understanding," I said, as I kissed the top of his head. I felt tears of relief and joy slipping down my cheeks. I didn't see or hear the office door opening. The receptionist had slipped in and left a package on the desk without speaking or disturbing us.

He looked at me and said: "I surmised you would want to finish what you started."

My dear friend's eyes twinkled as he opened the package and reached me the contents. I looked with amazement at bus tickets, timetables and an address of a small hotel. I couldn't speak. When my voice did come, I spluttered and stuttered like a child!

"You will phone me if you have any difficulties?" Mr Thompson's voice sounded shaky.

"I shall phone you every single day, difficulties or not!" I said as I planted another kiss on his plump cheek. Another chapter of my search into the past was about to begin. Tomorrow could not come too soon.

Chapter three

Countryside...

I arrived at the bus depot with time to spare. At such an early hour, I was surprised by the hive of activity. The noisy slamming of doors, revving engines and smell of diesel mixed with exhaust fumes, announced the start of another busy day in the city. From my seat in the waiting area, I watched the bustle that went on all around me.

Steady streams of people were in the process of boarding the waiting buses. I watched with interest the expressions on the many different faces, expressions that gave nothing away as to whether the journeys to be undertaken were business or pleasure. I looked at my watch. It was time to see if my transport was in its appointed place. It was. Minutes later I was seated beside a window, and my luggage with the exception of my small overnight case, had been loaded somewhere in the back. About twenty passengers filed in after me. From their casual dress I suspected they were tourists, or day-trippers. The sleeping engine of the bus came to life and we were on our way, as the large vehicle wound its way slowly along the narrow city streets, I once again had time to study my surroundings and the people. Tall brick chimneys belched thick grey smoke as men and women hurried through factory gates.

The bus slowed to almost walking pace as we reached the docks area. Ahead a sea of men, who followed one another like ants, walked in the direction of the shipyard, the many cloth capped workers flowed from the footpath and on to the road. I could just imagine all the impatient car drivers who were in a hurry.

The traffic and queues were soon forgotten as the bus sped along and out into the countryside. Farm hands were already at work in some of the fields, fields that up close were more beautiful than from the aeroplane. My eyes were beginning to smart from the early morning sunshine. It was only then that I realised my sunglasses were tucked up snug somewhere in the luggage. I rested my head against the back of the seat and listened to the steady whirring of the engine. Slowly my eyelids closed.

I awakened with a start. The engine, which had been like a lullaby to me, had stopped. My watch said my doze had lasted almost two hours. I wondered where we were and why we had stopped. I soon found out. Staring in the window were two of the most beautiful brown eyes I had ever seen, along with two soft ears and a mouth that seemed to be enjoying something tasty. I looked beyond one set of eyes and into more of the same. Cows! Unperturbed, the driver came sauntering down the aisle, announcing that there would be a short delay as this was market day in the nearby village.

"Does this happen often?" I asked innocently.

"No," he said jokingly. "Just on market days." I felt my face redden as he continued.

"You're not in the city now, Miss, things go a bit slower in this part of the world." With that he returned to his seat. He didn't give me a chance to even enquire which part of the world we were actually in.

The cows were in no hurry, but eventually we did get on our way. The countryside we were travelling through was dotted with small white cottages, not to mention sheep and cows by the hundreds. In the distance, a heavy mist hung like soft white candyfloss. I wondered what lay behind it - perhaps it hid the purple-topped mountains.

A short while later we arrived in a village. The bus stopped and up the aisle once more, sauntered the driver.

"Your stop Miss," he said. I was the only person who got off the bus. I was left standing on the roadside with my two suitcases, feeling like a lost animal.

'Where to now?' I inwardly panicked, as I walked across the dusty road to a small square surrounded by a cluster of cottages and shops.

"Miss Blackburn?" The voice came from behind me. I turned quickly to see a ginger-haired lad of about seventeen standing in front of me.

"Will you come with me, please?" he asked, as he lifted the cases.

I followed him like a lapdog across the road to one of the cottages.

"Here we are," he said, pushing open a red-painted door. I wanted to ask questions but developed cold feet. I just did as he asked and entered the house.

"Good day," a voice greeted me as I stepped from the bright daylight and into the misty greyness of a room. It took my eyes a few seconds to focus. The voice came again, this time with the face of its owner.

"Pleased to meet you. James McAuley's the name, and before you ask, Mr Thompson phoned me this morning!" I did eventually get around to asking a few questions, but not before this jovial man's rosy cheeked wife insisted I have a cup of tea.

Afterwards, I was shown to my bedroom. Like everything else in the small hotel, it was comfortable and homely.

"Dinner at six, Miss Blackburn," Mrs McAuley announced, in between telling me that I was the only guest, where the bathroom was, and a hundred and one other things. Much as I enjoyed her chatter, I was glad when she closed the door behind her. I needed half an hour to gather my thoughts. I unpacked and changed into comfortable jeans and a sweater.

'I won't be needing you for a while,' I said to my navy-blue suit as I hung it up in the wardrobe.

A few minutes later I sat down on the bed and looked around me. The little room was feminine and pretty, with floral wallpaper and matching bedspread. A gentle breeze filtered in through the open window, making the snowy-white curtains billow like sails on a boat. I crossed the room with the intention of closing it. As I drew back the curtains I went weak at the knees. There in all their glory were the mountains that Great Aunt Emily had loved. Once again, as in my mother's attic, a shiver went up my spine. I knew without a doubt that I was on Portmoley land. The only thing not in sight was the sea.

I felt dizzy with excitement as I made my way hurriedly downstairs for dinner. Mrs McAuley was in the dining room when I entered.

"Do you want to eat on your own, or with us?" she asked with a smile.

"With you please," I answered rather quickly. If Mrs McAuley noticed my eagerness, she showed no surprise as she carried on setting the table. More than anything I wanted to find out any small piece of information about this area, and what better place to start than with this pleasant couple?

Two hours later and after a dinner fit for royalty, all three of us sat around the blazing fire drinking our coffee. The landlord Mr James McAuley, simply known as McAuley, and his wife Margaret, were the most congenial company anyone could wish for. The talk, as they say flowed like good wine and it wasn't long before they heard my story. They couldn't tell me much except that this land had once belonged to the Blemmin family. They had been rich landowners and according to folklore, had owned all the land as far as the eye could see. The village itself had been here for hundreds of years.

The old graveyard, McAuley said, was just a lot of crumbling headstones that lay about five miles from the new church and its burial ground. I showed them the photo of the big house. Both studied it, but could tell me nothing. They listened with interest as I read the extract from the little book about the mountains and the sea. As I carefully wrapped my treasure in its cloth, I asked the question I had been dying to ask all evening.

"Where's the sea?"

"Just around the corner," McAuley smiled, as he puffed on his pipe.

Margaret explained just where 'around the corner' was!

"Do you fish?" her husband asked. I watched his face as he spoke.

"No but I'm willing to learn."

The broad smile on his face said I had given the right answer. I really wanted to go on with my search but it could wait another day.

I wasn't in any hurry to leave my new friends or this part of the world. It was almost midnight by the time I laid my head on the pillow. 'Too much coffee' was my last thought as I closed my eyes and snuggled deeper into a bed that was as soft as cotton wool.

The loud crowing of an early morning cockerel wakened me from a dreamless sleep. I screwed up my eyes and squinted at my watch. It said 6am, I turned over and pulled the quilt up around me in the hope I would go back to sleep. Unfortunately my brain was awake.

Slowly all the events that had happened in the last weeks paraded again before my eyes, starting in a dusty attic in Yorkshire and ending at this homely cottage in Ireland. It was unbelievable. My thoughts then turned to Cornwall, the farm and my beloved horses - how I missed my early morning rides. I wondered if McAuley knew of any riding stables. My musings were interrupted as a clock gave eight loud strikes. I literally jumped out of the bed. I had forgotten my promise to be ready for breakfast at 8:30pm.

Margaret was busy in the kitchen when I arrived downstairs.

"Mind if I come in?" I asked, peering around the door.

"Not at all Emily, your breakfast will be ready in two ticks."

She talked as she lifted a bowl of eggs and a frying pan at the same time.

"Himself is sorting out the rods and such for the trip and it looks like it's going to be another nice day." she said. Margaret chatted away and before long, she had set a plate in front of me. I looked at it in amusement and thought of the tea and toast I managed each morning.

"Eat up while I pack a picnic," she said, as she filled my teacup to the brim. McAuley entered the kitchen as I was finishing the last piece of ham. I had once again surprised myself and wondered where on earth my appetite came from.

"I'm ready when you are," he said, lifting the wicker basket, a bundle of keys and his pipe. I grabbed my anorak, woolly hat and trooped around behind him like a sheep dog. We stowed the rest of our gear into one of the oldest cars I had ever seen. I watched, fascinated as my smiling friend almost disappeared into the large boot and brought out a starting handle.

"Two turns of this and we'll be on our way." He laughed heartily as he settled me in the front seat of the vehicle. Margaret waved as the car gave two loud bangs then emitted a cloud of blue smoke.

"There we are, two turns is all that's needed," the proud owner said as he crunched up another gear.

The road was narrow and any idea of speed was out of the question. Travelling about twenty-five miles an hour gave me the chance to see up close the beautiful countryside. I saw fields with potato flowers in full bloom, some with corn and others where cows and sheep grazed, and others that ran riot with heather and wild flowers.

Around each bend there was always something to catch the eye. Beside me, my good friend kept up a running commentary on who owned the land and the animals. Suddenly the mountains came into view. I pointed without speaking.

"We're on the right side of them," McAuley smiled knowingly. My eyes never moved until we went around another bend.

"They'll be back. Don't worry," came his reassuring voice. A few minutes later he slowed the car down and pulled close to the verge of the road.

"Come on, Emily," McAuley's voice was full of excitement. "I want to show you something." I stepped out from the car quickly.

"Close your eyes and give me your hand." I did as he said and we both walked a few more yards.

"Stand here and when I count to three open your eyes," he said. Again, I duly did as he asked. I listened to his footsteps moving way and wondered what on earth had him so excited.

On his count of three I opened my eyes and blinked against the morning sun. Ahead of me lay fields of green, and surrounding them, the bright blue sea. The purple topped mountains were standing like great warriors protecting everything below. I let out a long deep gasp.

"Thought you'd like it," my friend said. I never answered. I just stood and stared. Never in my life, not even in beautiful Cornwall, was there anything to compare with the scene in front of me. I stood silent for a long time. It wasn't hard to imagine two people riding across the fields, or hear their laughter and whispers.

"Shall we move on?" My friend's concerned voice broke once more into my thoughts. I turned slowly from the little stone bridge I had been leaning against.

"Thank you, thank you a million times," I said. My voice was shaky and tears trickled down my cheeks.

"There, there, girl," McAuley's words tumbled out nervously. "Come on now, remember the fish won't wait all day you know!" I put my arms around his neck and gave him a hug!

In his own way he knew how I felt. We climbed into the car without another word. There was no need for conversation. Somehow, we both knew that talking would have broken the spell.

Half an hour later we arrived at a small harbour and within fifteen minutes, we were settled on board a fishing boat. McAuley caught most of the fish and I was more than happy to let him. He laughed, as did the other men at the shapes I managed to get into when I did catch one.

I was happy and relaxed in the company of my friend and his friends, but like all good things, the trip had to come to an end. We had been out for over three hours, but to me it seemed more like one. On the way home we talked about our day.

"Wait till I tell Mr Thompson tonight," I laughed. "I bet he'll never believe me, especially about eating a picnic in the middle of the sea!"

"He will," McAuley tittered. "It was his idea, a change from horses," he said. We were still laughing as we turned into the back yard of the small hotel. Margaret must have been patiently waiting for us. She opened the kitchen door and waved.

"Right on time!" she shouted, walking towards us. "The dinner's almost ready." I rushed from the car and gave her an unexpected hug.

"Wait until you hear about our day," I said, putting my arm around her shoulder. She looked across at her husband who stood with a smile on his face.

Dinner took longer than usual and it was my fault. I went into every small detail of our day, from beginning to end. When I described my special place, I could see from Margaret's face that her imagination was working overtime. Before our coffee stage of the evening, I said I would make a call to Mr Thompson and one to Joe, my farm manager.

"Take your time, the night's young!" McAuley shouted after me as he settled himself into an armchair.

As I set the receiver down, I could still hear the laughter of Mr Thompson at my first attempt at fishing. I was pleased he had information regarding the Blemmin family and their emigration to Australia. At least I would have another line of enquiry to follow when I returned. I hurried back to the sitting room and my waiting coffee.

"Everything's fine at the farm and Mr Thompson sends you both his regards," I said to the two people waiting. I then settled myself beside Margaret on the comfortable settee and as I had promised earlier, told her all she wanted to know all about the farm and my horses.

I had a captive audience and talked for almost an hour non-stop describing the farm, Cornwall and Yorkshire. Margaret asked many questions, whereas McAuley sat quietly puffing on his pipe.

"You can handle a horse then?" McAuley finally asked.

"I ride every day, summer or winter," I answered, then quickly added, "except for the last few weeks."

"It will come in handy." His voice came through another puff of smoke.

"What will?" Margaret inquired. McAuley continued as if he had never been interrupted.

"I was thinking there's a three-mile hike from old Glover's farm to the graveyard, riding will be easier than walking, old Tom has half a dozen good horses and Emily can take her pick."

He went on to say that given the directions, I could drive over in the car and then go the rest of the way on horseback.

"In the morning I'll draw up a map and give you a few tips on the car," he said. I sat with a smile on my face and said nothing. McAuley's smug look of satisfaction spoke for both of us.

"The end of a perfect day," I said picking up the cups and following Margaret into the kitchen.

"Goodnight Emily, sleep well," came the lilting chorus of two voices.

"Goodnight and thank you both once again," I said through a sleepy yawn. Before getting into bed, I opened the small window. The moon hung like a ball of silver in the night sky. I stood for a few minutes looking out into the dark stillness. I thought I heard small whispers, but I knew it was only the gentle breeze among the trees.

'I really am tired,' I said to myself as I climbed into bed. As I closed my eyes a thought came to me. *'If it was the breeze why did the curtains not move?'*

After breakfast the following morning all three of us sat around the table, studying the map that McAuley had sitting ready.

"It's a built-up area with plenty of new houses, so you can't miss it," he said. Margaret reminded me once again about the road ending at old Tom's farm. I listened to all their advice and instructions for the second time, including the fact that old Tom was expecting me.

"I'll finish making you a small lunch!" Margaret shouted over her shoulder as she headed towards the kitchen. "You go and change."

I looked in the mirror when I had finished dressing and was pleased with the results. I carried this outfit with me when I travelled. Sometimes I never used it, but there were times such as at horse sales and fairs when it was a blessing.

"What a professional!" Margaret and McAuley's words greeted me as I returned back to the kitchen. Margaret made me twirl around and around and loved what she called my trouser skirt. McAuley fancied the boots!

Ten minutes later the car engine was running smoothly. My two kind friends told me once more to be careful and not to stop until I got there. I shouted goodbye over the noise of the engine and then chugged slowly out of the yard. At last I was on my way.

The old car drove well. I kept my speed well down and enjoyed the scenery. The road was inland and I knew I would not come across the mountains or the sea, but at least I knew that this was the same ground that Emily had travelled over to meet her Samuel.

About an hour into my journey, houses started to appear, then into view came the spire of a church. I knew I was almost on the homeland of my ancestors. Somewhere around here, was where Emily had lived and died. More houses appeared, but not many. I drove slowly. Was this what McAuley called a built-up area? The buildings were mostly red brick, a complete contrast to the white cottages I had been used to just an hour's drive from here.

I continued on up the main road looking out for Tom Glover's farm. I couldn't have missed it if I had tried. I had just passed the last of the new houses when I spotted it, sitting on its own, surrounded by fields. Margaret had said it was where the road ended and she was right. An elderly man was standing at the front door as I parked the car.

"Morning, Miss," came his deep husky voice. I shook hands with him and wondered what to do or say next. I shouldn't have worried, because within seconds he ushered me indoors and put the kettle on to boil. If I thought McAuley could talk, I was wrong. Here was a man who could have beaten him hands down. An hour later I knew I had made another friend for life. After my second cup of tea I asked if I could see the horses.

"Thought you'd never ask," old Tom said, moving towards the door.

Out in the stable, just as McAuley said, were half a dozen horses. I chose a beautiful chestnut and saddled her up.

"Go straight, over the fields," Tom said, as he took something from his pocket, "and use these once the farm goes out of sight." I watched as he carefully tied a pair of binoculars securely to the saddlebag. I thanked him and mounted the horse.

With his words of 'take care now,' ringing in my ears, I turned and headed out into the countryside. Another part of my curiosity was about to be satisfied.

The horse, Star, was gentle and good-natured. I was in no hurry and wanted to enjoy the freeing openness of the fields and the smell of heather and wild flowers that drifted on the gentle breeze. I took my time, then slowly urged Star into a canter. The ground was heavy, but she took it in her stride. We moved along at a comfortable pace, giving a wide berth to the many groups of long-haired sheep, although I was sure Star was no stranger to them. As we approached another stone-built hedge, I noticed a small burn flowing along the side of it. I dismounted and let the horse drink from the cool, clear water, while I had a look through Tom's binoculars. In the distance I could just about make out the ruins of what I supposed was the old church. At least I knew we were heading in the right direction.

Star stood steady as I climbed back into the saddle. I gave her a couple of pats and then turned towards what I hoped would be my journey's end. The dot on the horizon grew bigger. Huge granite stones lay scattered over a wide area. I decided it would be safer to walk and lead the horse through them, rather than risk an injury to one of her legs. When we reached what I thought were the main ruins, I tethered the horse safely to a tree and started to make my way around the large stones. It took a few minutes to reach the graveyard. There was no proper gate, boundary or fence around it. It lay forgotten and alone behind another pile of boulders.

I felt like an intruder as I walked into the middle of the peaceful resting place. The only sound that came to my ears was the brushing of my skirt against the long grass and the occasional chirps of a lone bird. Carefully, I made my way around all the graves. I had hoped to see something, even a date, but the little graveyard held on tight to its secrets. All the crumbling markers were worn smooth with the passing of time. I felt slightly disappointed as I slowly turned and made my way back to Star. The horse looked content as she munched on a clump of fresh green grass. She heard me approach and just like a human, raised her head as if in welcome.

"I'm hungry too," I said giving her two or three pats on the rump. She answered with a flick of her tail. I took my lunch box from the saddlebag and then checked again that the horse was securely tethered. I decided to go back to the graveyard from the opposite direction, more out of nosiness than anything else.

I took one last look before heading back, and again, caught sight of the headstones from another viewpoint. It was then I noticed the patch of flowers almost hidden by more huge stones. Curious, I made my way around them and through another thick patch of long course grass. What can only be described as a miniature garden met my eyes. Beautiful wild roses scrambled madly over the rock face and into crevices. Wild flowers in a perfusion of colours swayed in the sunshine. They seemed to be making a statement about life in the middle of death. I stood mesmerised and unable to move. It was so beautiful I knew I would remember it all my life. I sat down on one of the stones. I was glad I had decided to come back and have another look before leaving. The moss on the stone was thick and as soft as velvet. I sat running my fingers through it for quite a long time.

'What better place than this to have your lunch?' I thought as I turned to lift the box. It was only then that I noticed the moss had peeled away from the stone and only seconds later when I too realised I was sitting on the edge of a headstone. I took the lid off the lunch box and scraped at the stone gently. Disbelief mixed with excitement made my heart beat fast. Slowly, I revealed the names Emily and Samuel.

I jumped up quickly. I stood trembling with all sorts of thoughts going through my head. Seconds later, I heard a voice call out my name. I turned quickly and was almost blinded by the sunlight, then through the brightness I made out the figure of a man.

"Who's there?" I shouted. The figure started moving towards me. I was gripped with panic and stepped back clumsily. I felt myself falling. Suddenly someone's arms were around me. I squealed and struggled, then everything went into slow motion and the sky seemed to fall on top of me.

The coldness on my brow made me open my eyes. A man was bending over me. I tried to get up but he gently pushed my shoulders back on the soft ground.

"Take it easy," he said, opening the top button on my jacket.

"What happened? Who are you?" I stammered.

"Take it easy," he said. "A few more minutes and we'll talk."

I lay back and watched the stranger as he poured something from a flask. There was something about him I couldn't quite figure out.

Ten minutes later I was propped up against a stone and accepting a cup of tea from this man I didn't know. Or did I?

"I'm sorry I frightened you," he said, lowering his head.

"I thought you were a ghost!" I laughed loudly. A smile spread over the stranger's face, and his eyes started to twinkle. It was then I remembered.

"Don't laugh. Wait until you see this," he said, reaching into his knapsack and taking out a photograph. He hesitated for a moment before reaching it to me.

"Great Aunt Emily!" I exclaimed. "How on earth? Where did you?" I was stopped in mid-sentence by his great loud whoops and cheers.

'I knew it, I just knew it!' He gave another cheer.

"Are you related to the Blemmins?" I asked. He stopped laughing and looked at me. Before he answered I knew he was.

Almost an hour later we were still talking. I couldn't really take in everything he told me and neither could he, when I told him my side of the story.

"Grandma, it's almost time to go home." The sweet lilting voice of my granddaughter brought me back from my daydreams.

"Coming," I answered, closing my book.

"Another chapter, Mum?" I looked up again, this time at the questioning face of my daughter.

"Yes Emily, and it seems like only yesterday that I started to record all the happenings in these," I said, running my hand over one of my three precious journals. She smiled and I saw again her father's twinkling eyes.

"Ten more minutes and we'll set off for home," she said as she gathered up the remains of our picnic lunch.

I sat back and enjoyed the perfume of the flowers. It was hard to believe that thirty years had passed since Sam and I had met here. McAuley and Margaret couldn't believe it when I arrived back with a stranger that night. All of us found it more than a coincidence that two people living only sixty miles apart in England should find each other in a graveyard in Ireland. Sam had to repeat all he told me, to them.

He explained how ten years had passed since he first started coming to Ireland on a hitch-hiking holiday and also to look for his namesake and great uncle's grave. I sat wide-eyed once more, listening to how he decided to leave the headstone where it lay when he planted the flowers, and how his great Uncle Samuel had died of a broken heart a year after Emily died. The family carried out their son's last request to be buried with her.

Sam said that most of his uncle's letters, books and papers were lost and the very little that remained, was passed down through the family until they came to him, the last surviving relative in the Blemmin family. The lineage in Australia had ended when the only other son returned to England and he, as we learned, was Sam's grandfather James.

Out of all the papers there was just the one photograph of Emily and a letter that spoke of Portmoley, her love of horses and their forth-coming marriage. When Sam showed the photograph to my friends, they understood why he had mistaken me for a ghost. I had to admit there was a strong resemblance.

My memory flitted back again over everything that had happened from that night - our wedding, dear old Tom leaving us his farm when he died, our move to Ireland. Then Sam, becoming the rector of the parish church and sharing our beloved horses, the birth of our daughter completing and blessing our life of happiness and contentment.

Memories - hundreds and hundreds of memories. Over the years I had written them all down so that my daughter and granddaughter would always remember how Sam and I first met. They were memories of our early days and the love that we shared. I looked around once more at the sea of flowers. It had taken Sam and myself almost ten years to finally finish restoring the little graveyard from a wilderness into a haven of beauty. It was a labour of love carried out in memory of two special people. Two people who, for a brief period loved each other, and in a strange way entered our lives to bring Sam and me together.

"Ready, Mum?" My daughter shouted. I knew by her voice she was growing impatient. Then suddenly I remembered why. Two new horses were arriving at 4pm and she was anxious to see them.

"Yes Emily, coming now," I said, lifting my bag and moving closer to the headstone. I touched it lovingly.

"Soon, Sam," I said quietly. "I'll be back soon." I walked slowly along the tidy gravel path, turned and looked back. The memory of our parting three years ago still caused me heartache and pain.

A tear came to my eye as I felt a gentle softness drifting into my face and ruffling my grey curly hair.

"How did your hair get tossed?" Emily asked, as I approached the car. "It's so hot there's not even a breeze, let alone a wind!"

"Something's in the air!" I said, glancing backwards…

Perception...

Moving on...

I'm sure like me, you can think of a few things that are stressful; top of my list has to be moving house! In 1960, my husband was employed in Belfast; our decision to relocate was made easy by his early starts and late homecomings. Packing up our bits and pieces didn't take long; our belongings were so small that the cost of a removal van was not on the agenda. My grandmother came to the rescue, she had a friend whose son drove a lorry on a regular basis to Belfast; he was happy to oblige.

The morning the removal van arrived, I felt my face growing as red as a boiled beetroot. The driver and his flatbed lorry, delivered flour from a Ballymena flour mill to bakeries in Belfast; the remains of the last delivery was still obvious, as the boards on the lorry's bed were still white! I was so glad our move happened on a sunny day, as the lorry came minus a tarpaulin, I dreaded to think what our belongings would have looked like, if rain had mixed with the flour!

We spent many happy years in our little home; when the time came for us to relocate again, I made sure the removal van had a roof and closed in sides!

All of us have, or will be caught up in a *different move* at one time or other in our lives. This *moving on* could be the loss of our job, retirement, illness or the death of a loved one. Moves that can bring heartache and pain.

In the Bible we read of Naomi and Ruth, they too had to move on. They left Moab and travelled to Bethlehem. Before they left, Ruth made the decision to change her birth faith to that of Naomi's. They had very little money and just a few possessions; the heaviest thing they carried was the pain in their heart. When they reached Bethlehem it was the start of the barley harvest, to them it was a blessing and they could find work. It was the first blessing of many for two widow women who put all their trust and faith in God.

We, like these two Biblical women, need to trust God when any move comes into our lives. In this little poem I have tried to look at Ruth's thoughts as she left her homeland.

Ruth Ch. 1 'Naomi and Ruth return to Bethlehem'

Moving On...

I lifted my bundle and turned one last time
The room was eerie, barren and cold,
Gone now the warmth and homely touch, swept clean of love,
And dreams that fade in earthly dust…

At the crossroads we lingered, three women in widows weeds
Orpah clung tightly as we kissed goodbye,
From a treetop a songbird's sad mantra rose high in the sky
A mantra for parting, teardrops and sighs…

What will greet us in Bethlehem Town?
For an exile – disgrace. For a stranger - no place,
Chin wagging, laughter, scorn
No pity for two penniless women, bereft and alone…

Wearily we walked, my hood pulled down in the noonday heat
I didn't see the olive trees with fruit red and green… until,
A breeze tugged at my cloak and then touched my cheek
A breeze that carried the smell of barley, and golden eared wheat…

It was when Naomi reached for my hand… that I knew
This good woman, so low in spirit, was in her homeland,
We stood in silence, as the breeze tugged and swirled all around
Until, the last dust of Moab was swallowed… by Judean ground…

Yes, I have moved on, where Naomi sleeps I will there lay my head
Her land is my land, her God will be my God and I trust and believe,
The Great God of Israel
Will bless and guide, Naomi and me…

STORY XII

Woolly Friend's

'A champion named Goliath, who was from Gath, came out of the Philistine camp. His height was six cubits and a span.'

1 Samuel 17:4

"Will I sing you a song?" I asked the crowd. They looked at me and kept on eating. I watched their mouths, they kept on chewing. I wondered if I kept eating all day, would I grow tall and strong like my seven brothers.

I loved the sheep and I loved the hillside, but sometimes, I wanted to go with my three eldest brothers and stay with them in the fighting fields. I had been there before and played my harp for the king and my brothers. No one, not even the king would let me stay more than a day. I was always sent back to the sheep. I pushed these thoughts to the back of my mind and lifted my harp. My woolly friends gathered around me.

"Be quiet now," I said to the chewing mouths. The sheep ignored me and kept on chewing. I played and sang and they joined in with their loud bleats. What a din we created.

"David, David!" The cross voice of my brother brought our musical gathering to a halt. He started laughing.

"You will never teach them to sing!" he said.

We both laughed; then my brother said: "You have to return home."

My father met us at the gate.

"Come David, this man wants to see you," he said as he ushered me in through the door.

The man was very old. He prayed as he poured oil on my head.

"This is the one," he said, to my anxious looking father. They talked quietly. I wiped a drop of oil from my eye and wondered why they looked so serious.

"Can I go back to the sheep?" I asked. My father looked strained and worried.

"Not today," he replied. "I need you to go on an errand."

The old man left.

"David, I am worried about your brothers, I want you to take these provisions to the camp," said my father. I looked at the assortment of food and wondered if I could carry it all.

I set off early the next morning. A few hours later I was standing in the middle of the noisy encampment. I left the food with the cook and went to find my brothers. They were happy to see me and said they were looking forward to the home-made food. I was about to tell them about the old man, when a troop of soldiers came running over the hill.

"It's Goliath!" they shouted.

"He wants someone to fight him," said one of the soldiers. My brothers hurriedly lifted their swords and spears. I was told to go home.

"Please can I stay?" I asked. Their answer was the same as before, only louder.

"Go home, go now!" they shouted. I said goodbye to my brothers and pretended to leave the camp. I wanted to see the man who had everyone running in fear. I dodged between tents and horses, and hid below the front wheel of a cart.

I could see the big fighting man. He was at least nine feet tall and was carrying the largest sword I had ever seen. Unfortunately, at that moment my brothers spied me. They were so cross. They once again ordered me home. I refused and said I wanted to fight Goliath. They laughed and cuffed me on the head.

Just then a guard arrived. He had told King Saul I was willing to fight. A few minutes later I was in the king's tent.

The king argued that I was little more than a boy. I told him I had fought off lions and bears, and I wanted to fight Goliath. Finally he agreed, providing I wore his armour. I tried it on, but I couldn't walk.

"I will go as I am, the Lord will protect me," I said. The king didn't argue as he nodded his head. I left the tent and made my way to a small stream. I knew what I needed. I picked up five smooth stones. I was ready to meet the big man.

I stood looking at the tyrant. He looked at me and started to laugh.

"Are you the only one Saul could send?" he asked, waving his sword.

I shouted back, "The true God is on our side!" I had my sling and stones in my hand. I waited a few moments then aimed at his head. For a moment he looked at me and then fell to the ground with a loud thud. I knew he was dead before I approached his body. I did what I always do with wild animals, I cut off his head. Within minutes my brothers and the soldiers were at my side.

Shouts of '*You did it David, you have saved us all!*' filled the air, as they hoisted me onto my brothers' shoulders and marched back to the camp.

So much has happened since I first stood on the battlefield. Over the years I have made good and sincere friends, and some wicked ones. The one friend, who was and is ever true, is my God. To Him I turn in happy times and sad. I feel humble as I step out in the robes and crown of kingship. I, who was a shepherd and not born of royal blood. Sometimes being a king is a lonely job.

At times like today, when my head is filled with decision making, I leave ruling and slip away to the quietness of the hillside. Here I can forget for a few hours and once more become a shepherd. I play the harp and sing. The sheep still crowd around me, and as always, they keep eating and bleating.

I smile when I think of what my brother said that day.

"You will never teach them to sing," he said. I looked at my woolly companions. It's true they will never sing, but they do listen and sometimes that's all a shepherd or a king needs...

STORY XIII

The Birthday Party

'Those who want to get rich fall into temptation and a trap and into many foolish and harmful desires that plunge people into ruin and destruction.'

1 Timothy 6:9

It was the birthday party of the year and I had been chosen to be one of the serving maids. I was apprehensive about what lay ahead of me. I had provided my services to lower dignitaries, but the worry of being in the same company as a high-ranking governor sent shivers up my spine.

Worse still was his wife. In the kitchen we called her *a sharp old goat*. She was demanding and hostile. Her daughter was not much better. She was arrogant, self-assertive and thought everyone was there to do her bidding.

These thoughts quickly left my mind as my three friends and I were called to the kitchen. The party was about to begin. I lifted a large jug of wine and followed my friends into the noisy function room. Some of the lavishly-dressed guests were already tipsy, especially the men, their coarse language and sneers reminded me to neither speak nor smile. Many times I had been warned by my mother of the underhand treacheries of the upper-class. As I listened and watched the company I was serving, I understood why she said what she did.

The function room was full to capacity and I was kept busy refilling the fast emptying goblets. Then without warning, an unexpected blare of horns was heard. Then came the announcement: "Make way for the King." I stood transfixed at the scene before me. There, in all their finery were the most important and influential people in the land.

As the dignitaries sat down, a troop of dancing girls moved onto the floor. All eyes were now on them, including mine! The dancer with their bejewelled hands and feet, tantalizing dresses and tambourines, twisted and twirled like a multi-coloured breeze through the throng of overexcited people. I had to force myself to move on to the next empty goblet!

A few minutes later I was serving close to the royals and their family. I overheard part of a conversation between the governor and his daughter.

"Please dance for me," he said to her.

She laughed and replied, "At a price."

It was at that moment I was called to another table. I didn't hear any more of the discussion and to be honest, I wasn't really interested.

Two hours later when everyone had feasted on the sumptuous food, the empty goblets were in need of refilling. I was moving from guest to guest when suddenly the governor stood up and announced his daughter was going to dance. The room fell silent. Everyone's head turned to the sheer gold hangings at the door. Soft music came from the lyres; then from behind the drapes came the dancer. Everyone gasped. Her dress was made of delicate scarlet shawls. The cloth was so flimsy that we all could see she was wearing very little underneath.

She swayed slowly and provocatively across the floor and stopped short of her step-father.

"Anything?" she asked, as she moved closer.

"Anything for you," he answered, as his hand wiped the sweat from his brow.

His step-daughter writhed and twirled on the floor like a wild animal. It was not a normal dance - it was teasing and seductive in every way. Some of the uncouth remarks coming from the men made me feel uncomfortable.

My friends and I looked and felt embarrassed. While everyone else clapped and cheered, the men were the loudest of all. Minutes later the music ended and the dance was over.

I then had to take more wine to the top table. As I placed the fresh flask of wine beside the king's goblet, I heard his raised voice. He and his daughter were embroiled in a heated argument. I moved away quickly. He was angry when he spoke and he looked annoyed. His daughter was laughing.

The party was drawing to a close when two guards marched through the door. They placed a silver tray before King Herod Antipas, his wife Herodias and step-daughter Salome.

I watched as the lid was slowly lifted. Gasps of horror came from the guests. I moved closer to the royal group. What I saw made we retch. I felt faint. It was like a bad dream. On the tray in a pool of blood, was the head of a man I knew. The man was John the Baptist…

I left the palace that night in the knowledge I would never return. I could never look at the faces that had put an innocent preaching man to death. He was a simple man, a man who didn't even own a decent cloak, a man who lived by the river; a man who loved God.

I learned a few weeks later how this tragedy happened and why it happened. It was also about that time I first met John's friend and cousin, Jesus. His teaching on love and forgiveness touched and changed my angry, bitter heart into one of compassion.

I am thankful, thankful that I found Jesus and His everlasting love.

Each night I pray that God will have mercy and forgive a foolish king, his devious wife and step-daughter…

ANTICPATION

STORY XIV

A worried man...

Going on holiday and staying in a hotel sounds great. No more cooking, washing or bed-making for two weeks - fantastic! Getting away on holiday means planning and booking flights, and finding a good hotel is top priority.

By the time everything is arranged and paid for, we really need the holiday! It's the same when going on a journey, short or long, planning is required.

A long time ago, a couple I know set out on a journey. There was some planning involved, but not enough. The couple arrived at their destination but forgot to book bed and breakfast. They wandered around the town, searching here and there, but to no avail. All the boarding houses were full and not one had a vacancy sign in the window.

Perhaps some of you have been in that sorry situation and have lived to tell the tale. If you have a few minutes, listen to this man's story. He will tell you how his journey ended in a busy, jam-packed town.

A Worried Man...

I sighed as I saw the first flickering lights of the town. This had been a long drawn out journey. I was glad it was almost at an end. Perhaps I should have allowed more time. Perhaps we should have had the company of others. Why did I not plan ahead?

My feet are sore; my head aches with thoughts of things I don't quite understand. I love my sweet wife, and I will love the baby soon to be born.

It's a blessing the donkey is sure-footed, and needs little prodding to hurry it along. Another few miles…

My uneasy thoughts were interrupted by my wife's anxious voice.

"Hurry, please hurry," she said.

Time after time, I tied the weary donkey to the railing of large and small rooming houses. Time after time, I was greeted with the same answer, *'sorry.'* I was desperate; my wife was almost in tears. I had reached the end of the main road with all hope of lodgings gone. I pulled my hood over my head and trudged on. My eyes were stinging from the dust and gritty sand, as I wiped them I almost missed the small lane to the left of the road. Carefully I guided the donkey in the darkness, ahead of me I saw a small dim light, then a building. It looked deserted but I could see wisps of smoke coming from the chimney.

The wavering light above the door allowed me to see the word '*Inn*.' My hopes were raised until I read the notice pinned to the entrance door, '*Full Up, No Room.*' I ignored the notice and knocked loudly.

Three times I knocked, no one answered. I knocked once more, this time the knock was so loud it sent tiny mice scampering from their nest. I listened, then I heard muttering from behind the large door. My heart was beating fast as a bolt was drawn and then the latch lifted. I could just about see a tousle-haired man, with one foot pressed against the door.

"Please," I started to say, but he angrily cut me off with his cross words.

"We're full, can't you read?"

I tried again, but he wouldn't listen. He was about to close the door but then he stepped outside and looked at the pathetic sight before him. A dust covered man, a weary donkey and a very pregnant woman. He looked uneasy as he asked, "Would the byre do?"

I thanked him for his kindness.

"Wait here," he said abruptly, closing the door in my face. We waited. A few minutes later he returned with a lamp and blankets. We followed him in silence.

The byre smelled of foul sweat, but it was warm. Quickly I made a bed from the fresh hay and laid blankets over it. The baby was about to be born.

I wrapped our son in a homespun blanket and laid Him close to his mother. I gazed with wonder at our first-born child. I touched His tiny perfect hands. He was so beautiful. Mary's eyes met mine and for a moment this baby was ours. The moment passed, as we both recalled all that had happened over the past few months.

This child was not our child - he was God's Son. My mind was crowded with thoughts. I was just a man, a simple man, a carpenter, yet I was chosen by God to be His Son's earthly father. Tears streamed down my cheeks. I was afraid. I knelt down and gazed again at this special child. Tears came again, tears of gratitude, as peace flooded my soul. Our God had wiped all fear from my heart. I was at peace. God had honoured me above all men. I felt humble as I placed another rug over the makeshift bed, a bed where a mother and child lay in contented sleep. One journey had ended. In my heart I felt a new one was about to begin…

STORY XV

A Landlord's Dilemma

A few years ago I was returning from a much-needed holiday. I was feeling on top form and was looking forward to settling back into my routine of being the typical busy wife and mother. Unfortunately, when I arrived at the airport, the pilots and handling staff had called a lightning strike. Hundreds of irate passengers were milling around. Some of the travellers were being *very* rude to the receptionists.

"Where will we stay?" "Get the supervisor!" And, "We want a refund!" Were the demands coming from the frustrated crowd as they moved about like flustered eagles.

The people calmed down when an airport director arrived. The soft-spoken man assured us, that accommodation would be provided in different hotels. Half an hour later, I joined around thirty others at the door of a smallish hotel, only to be greeted with the words, "sorry, we can't take any more."

The *eagles* showed their feathers again and demanded to see the manager. He arrived. He listened; then tried to explain that all the rooms were full.

"Try somewhere else!" he shouted. The booing became louder. By now the children in the crowd were hungry and most of them were in tears. The manager held up his hands. Everyone stopped what they were doing and waited for him to speak.

"I can offer you all a bed in the basement, but you will have to share it with the utilities," he said. I slept that night beside a huge silent washing machine.

The following morning the strike was over. We were all smiling as we boarded the plane for home. Later that day, as I removed grains of sand from my suitcase, I thought again of the hotel manager. He was in a difficult position, he couldn't give what he didn't have, and for a moment he was at his wit's end. Then he offered a poor alternative and was surprised when the offer was accepted. All this brings to mind another hotelier, he too was in a difficult position and he too offered a poor substitute for a room.

If you have a moment, this landlord will tell you of that night…

A Landlord's Dilemma…

I dropped the latch on the door and let out a sigh of relief. Most of my guests were in bed asleep and the latecomers were tossing and turning. The floor was not the most comfortable place to sleep but these latecomers were glad to find any type of shelter indoors. The nights here were cold and tonight was no exception.

With everyone almost settled and the sign firmly attached to the door, it was my turn to have a well-earned rest. I could almost feel the comfort that awaited me beside the fire, but first I had to squeeze myself between a sleeping child and a pile of blankets to enjoy it.

I eased myself into the well-worn, but comfortable chair. As I bent down to untie my sandals, the heat from the fire brought niggling thoughts. I felt pity for anyone who was not indoors tonight.

The heat from the embers was comforting. I was cosy, content and almost asleep when a loud, persistent knocking startled me. I decided to ignore it. The knocking went on and on. I didn't move. I hoped whoever was there would go away. Some of my floor-sleeping guests began to stir when the thumping grew louder.

I became annoyed and grumpy as I once again squeezed past the sleeping bodies. Whoever was at the door must be drunk. As I lifted the latch and put one foot between the door and the doorpost, my intention was to be rid of the nuisance as quickly as possible.

Through the small opening I saw a weary and distressed man. I opened the door a bit further and in the shadowy light I saw a pitiful sight. It was a woman with her head bent low, leaning against a donkey. She didn't look well. The man's pleading touched my heart but I had no other choice but to refuse. Where on earth could I put them? The man gave me one last heart-rending look before he turned away. Why do people not take notice of notices? What's the point of putting them up if they still thump the door?

I was cold, tired and feeling grumpy again. I had just stepped inside and was about to close the door when something made me hesitate and call out.

"There is the stable!" I shouted. I didn't expect the man to accept, let alone the woman. I was taken aback when not once, but twice the man thanked me. I muttered something about finding my sandals and needing to fetch a lamp.

Ten minutes later I returned. The woman had moved out of the shadows, and it was then I saw the strain on her face, caused by the fact that she was pregnant. I was just an innkeeper, but even I could tell the birth would happen soon. I led the weary couple the short distance to the stable, offered them clean straw and a few blankets; then I quickly left.

As I made my way back to the house, the lamplight flickered in the night breeze. Yes, it was going to be another bitterly cold night. Once again, I dropped the latch and once again, I made my way to my old comfortable chair.

At least, I thought, as my eyelids closed, two more people and a bedraggled donkey are in from the cold…

STORY XVI

Promise and Joy

Our only daughter was born in 1973 - that was also the year of the big snow. I'm sure many of you will remember that year. It snowed and snowed for days on end. Everything was disrupted - gas and electricity supplies were cut off, railways, roads and airports were closed.

Where we lived, there were no deliveries of coal or milk. It was on such a night that my daughter decided it was time to enter the world.

The midwife was called, as was the doctor, but both of their cars were immovable due to the snow, which meant coming on foot. My husband decided to collect the midwife as she lived just a mile away, but not before spending fifteen minutes digging our car out of a snow drift.

Everything turned out fine and within fifteen minutes, with the nurse at my side, our baby was born. The doctor arrived on foot an hour later looking like a walking snowman. A hot cup of tea and a slice of Christmas cake set both of them up for their cold walk home.

A bitterly cold night brings to mind another birth and the unease of a first-time mother. Her story has been retold countless times - perhaps you would like to read it once more…

Promise and Joy

The byre door creaked and slammed behind us, almost blowing out the light from the small lamp. It took a few moments for my eyes to be become accustomed to the shadowy darkness. My nostrils rebelled at the smell of the animals and the sweaty, steamy heat that clung to the air. I felt sick. I was so afraid. I wanted to cry out for my mother.

My dear husband, so patient and caring, guided me to a space against a wall. I leaned against its coldness; then pressed my face to a crack between the stones. The sharp night air was like the cool touch of my mother's hand. I watched my husband as he quickly gathered clean hay into a pile and then spread a few blankets over it.

I tried to keep the angel's words in my mind as Joseph wiped the sweat from my brow. How I loved Joseph for his understanding, his trust and his belief in me. From tear-filled eyes, I watched him moving about. I heard the restlessness of the animals.

Then came that great pain. Moments later, another sound came to my ears, a sweet sound, my child's first cry. My first-born child, my little son. Joseph wrapped him in a blanket and laid him close to me. We both touched his tiny hands and feet - how we loved our baby. For a moment this child was ours, our dearest son. Then as our eyes met, we both seemed to become as one, our thoughts merging as we remembered the angel's words.

We had come so far in faith. We would keep on trusting in our God. We smiled at each other; then kissed the downy head of a baby, a baby given to us for safe keeping, God's Son come to earth.

Joseph stood gazing at our child for a few more minutes. Then tears started rolling down his cheeks. I let him be. He had his own thoughts. I knew he had been under a great strain since we left Nazareth. The distress of no lodgings, the many times doors were slammed in his face, yet this dear man never complained.

I drifted in and out of sleep as Joseph tidied our belongings and fed our weary donkey. I looked once more at the child lying beside me - the Son of God was asleep. I brought Him closer to my breast and closed my eyes. God had kept his promise. My heart was filled with joy and like my sleeping child, I was content...

The Travellers...

Today most families own a car. When I was a child, some families were considered very fortunate if they owned a bicycle! Living in a small town, cars were not really needed as we had so many shops within a stone's throw from our homes. In one small triangle we had two butchers, four grocers, a shoe-mender, a chemist and two dairies to mention just a few. Anyone who needed to journey to the town shops went by way of Shanks pony!

Cars were a rarity. There was a taxi man but his service was seldom needed; when one was needed, people had to go to the saw-mill to find him, the poor man had to work, he needed a wage just like everyone else. The one man, who found it easy to make his take-home pay, was the shoe-mender; it is easy to see why!

We did have buses and trains; the train was generally used to haul heavy goods to the city. However, once a year it carried a different load; it was always packed to capacity, its destination the seaside. It was our annual Sunday school trip. The sound of laughter poured out from the carriages of the train, a train that shunted and puffed out of the station carrying excitement and hundreds of buckets and spades.

I wonder how many of you have ever been on a mystery tour. As a child I found these journeys great fun; guessing where we were going to was our favourite game. With the blinds on the bus pulled down we would wait patiently for the driver to shout out, "we've arrived," and regardless of where the mystery tour took us, we always enjoyed ourselves.

We read in the Bible of some men that set out on the greatest of mystery tours. They had no bus or car to travel in, however, they did have an unusual escort, but not one that shouted out, *"we've arrived!"* Their escort was a star and its voice came from its bright shining light. They trusted the star, always keeping in mind, that at the end of their journey they would meet a child born to be a King.

When the star stopped and shone brightly over a stable in little Bethlehem, these learned men knew their long mystery journey was over. They had trusted in a guiding star and the star knew exactly where to take them…

The Travellers…

When we heard of the star and its reason for being
We knew it was time to go searching and seeking,
We'd been promised from days of old
A holy one to be born here on earth,
And Israel His place of his birth.

Many months ago we set out from home
And followed the star wherever it roamed,
It guided us through barren lands
Up hills, down dales, into valleys so green,
Until, we became like deep sleepers chasing a dream.

Onward and onward we followed the star
Then one night near King David's town,
Its light grew so bright and shone all around
 We were confused as we searched here and there,
And agreed, this place wouldn't do for Gods Son and Heir.

We had searched for a palace with soldiers on guard
Instead, we found a stable in an innkeepers' yard,
The owner was amazed when our story he heard
He gave us a lamp and quietly said,
"You have my permission to enter the shed."

We went in expecting to see
Rich silken robes around the babe's head,
And soft woven rugs on His tiny bed
But what we found,
Made us hold our breath and utter no sound.

In a manger of sweet-smelling hay
Peacefully sleeping
The child-King lay,
As we laid our gifts on the straw covered ground
They seemed as nothing to the treasure we found.

Days and nights passed, how we wanted to stay
But we knew of danger in following days,
As we started out from that little town
The last rays of sun-shine came cascading down,
Bethlehem became as a diamond, in a king's jewelled crown.

As we travelled on we knew we'd been blessed
On that holy night God granted we three,
The splendour of His Son
Content where He lay,
Asleep… in a crib of sweet-smelling hay…

STORY XVII

The Eyes of a King

'For a child will be born to us, a son will be given to us; And the government will rest on His shoulders; And His name will be called Wonderful Counsellor, Mighty God, Eternal Father, Prince of Peace.'

Isaiah 9:6

My mother was at it again. Fussing! Three times that day she had told me, "Don't stray from your brothers, stay by their side and keep your cloak wrapped tightly around you."

I wanted to say, "I am eight years old, not four!" I loved my mother and I knew she was worried about my first night on the hillside. I, on the other hand, was thrilled to be out at night, when friends the same age as me would be in bed asleep.

It was about 10 o'clock when my two brothers James and Jacob lifted their staffs. I knew without being told that my night adventure was about to begin. James repeated my mother's words.

"Ben," he said. "Don't wander away. Keep close to us and you will be alright." I nodded my head in agreement, as I walked proudly beside him. Half an hour later we had left the flat dirt road and were now on a gentle climb.

"Nearly there," James said, as he moved his leather bag from one shoulder to the other.

Jacob rubbed his hands and said, "It's going to be another cold night, look at the stars Ben, see how sharp and bright they are." I locked this piece of information in my head. If I was going to be a shepherd, I needed every scrap of information I could get.

The tinkling of bells and a few low bleats told me we were close to the flock. Within minutes we were surrounded by a crowd of bleating sheep. I giggled as they nudged our cloaks. James told me the sheep knew who we were.

"A bit like our dogs," he said. "They know our smell." More information for my head.

Jacob, meanwhile, was busy placing stones in a small circle, James was unpacking his bag. I was told to collect wood for the fire. I felt pleased as I returned with an armful of sticks.

"That's not kindling," James said laughing, as he lifted a small handful of dry moss. More information! I wondered how much more I needed. Ten minutes later and the fire was well ablaze. James had returned from a nearby stream with a full waterskin. He poured oats, honey and water into a pot and set it on the crackling fire. It was soon ready and we all tucked into our midnight meal.

"Ben, always make sure the sheep are close to water, they like us need to drink, as well as eat," Jacob said.

James pointed to our empty plates. "No water, no meal," he said.

I was beginning to think there was more to this type of job than I thought.

The night air was becoming icy. I drew my cloak around me and covered my head with my hood. The heat from the fire, the soft light from our lanterns and a full tummy, had me blinking and rubbing my eyes. James told Jacob that he would take the first watch. Another question was on my lips. Before I could ask, he said, "Wild animals, Ben, wolves and bears."

I shuddered as he continued, "remember what I said; stay close to Jacob." I pulled another blanket around my shoulders, looked at Jacob and then closed my eyes. I knew I'd be safe with my brother.

I don't know how long I slept, but I do know I was shaken awake by Jacob.

I thought it was daytime - there was light everywhere.

James came running towards us.

"What is it Jacob?"

"I don't know," he answered in a shaky voice. I stood between them trembling. The light got brighter, so bright we all had to cover our eyes. I felt hot tears on my cheek. I wanted my mother.

Slowly the bright light changed to a mist. In the middle of it was a man. I blinked and rubbed my eyes. The man was dressed in the whitest of white flowing robes. I rubbed my eyes again, not believing what I had seen. The man had wings!

My brothers gasped and fell on their knees.

James pulled me close, and whispered, "It's an angel." I was so scared. Then within seconds we were all in the centre of the mist. The angel spoke softly.

"Don't be afraid, I mean you no harm," he said. I lifted my eyes and looked at his shining face. He was beautiful. He pointed to the night sky and then spoke again.

"This star will lead you to a stable in Bethlehem. Go and see the Baby. He will be a King." I looked at my brothers. They were nodding their heads. I turned to the man and nodded my head too. Suddenly the angel was gone and the mist slowly faded.

In the dark night sky was one of the brightest stars I had ever seen. All three of us stood in silence; then Jacob said, "We must go." The three of us worked quickly. James filled the water troughs for the sheep, Jacob packed our belongings and I doused the fire with the remaining water. We left the hill and the sheep. I walked quietly beside my two brothers and wondered what we would find in Bethlehem.

Our eyes never left the star until we arrived back in the sleeping town.

"Where to now?" Jacob asked, as he pulled up his hood.

"Jacob, look over there - the star has stopped over there!" I said, jumping up and down with excitement!

We slowly wound our way along a few narrow streets. The star never moved. As we turned a corner we saw the boarding house.

The star still didn't move. James took a lantern and walked quietly up the side of the house. We waited. He came back quickly.

"Come," he said. "We have found a stable."

We went quietly in through the byre door. In the dim light of our lanterns we could see cattle and sheep, their breath forming steam clouds in the cold night air. A donkey stood in a corner. It looked at us; then swished its tail as we passed.

We moved further into the bleak building. James lifted his lantern higher. It was only then we saw the two people. The woman was resting on a blanket, the man was kneeling beside her; close to them was a straw-filled crib. We moved a few more steps and then we saw the Baby - the Baby the angel said was a King. His little body was covered with soft blankets. We knelt before His humble bed. I thought the Baby had the sweetest face and beautiful eyes. But I couldn't see any jewels or a crown. Just a Baby.

As we made our way home that night, my brothers told me the Baby's name was Jesus and that His father had spoken about all the happenings even before His birth. For a moment I found this information hard to believe, but then, I did believe I'd seen an angel, and then there was the bright shining star. Perhaps little Jesus was a very special child. I trusted my brothers and if they believed He was a King, then I believed too.

It was almost daylight when Jacob tucked me into bed. I was still thinking about the Baby, the angel and the star.

"Do you think we will ever see the Baby King again?" I asked with a yawn. Both of my brothers answered as one, "Yes, Ben, we will see Jesus again."

Thirty years have passed since that night. My wife and I now live on the outskirts of Jerusalem. My two brothers still live near Bethlehem and are still herding sheep on the hills. I too became a shepherd, although it took years of training with my brothers to become one. Many times, especially at night on the dark hills of Jerusalem, the memory of that one special night would come back to me.

I often wondered what had become of the Baby. Then, as soon as daylight appeared I would forget everything and hurry home to bed.

That was how it was this morning, only I wasn't going home. I had to go to the opposite side of the city to order leather.

Jerusalem was already packed to capacity when I arrived. I took a shortcut, only to be met by more crowds of people. They weren't going anywhere. They stood in a tight throng listening to a preaching man. I tried to push my way through the crowd but I was trapped in the middle and like it or not, I too was going nowhere.

I resigned myself to listening to the talk around me.

'He healed a blind man. He made a crippled man walk, He talks of God and peace on earth.' I stood listening as people told of the many healings carried out by the preacher. By now I was eager to hear more about the man.

"Who is He?" I asked the woman beside me.

She stared at me in surprise, then said, "You must be a stranger, everyone knows Jesus."

The woman paused for a moment, then said, "Many people say He's the King, others say He's the Son of God." Her words brought memories rushing back to my mind.

I pushed my way through the crowd, until I was almost in front of the preacher. He stopped talking and looked straight at me. His eyes searched my face.

"Can I help you?" He asked. For a moment I couldn't speak. My mouth was dry. I fumbled for words; then I asked, "Were you born in Bethlehem?"

He smiled as He laid His hand on my shoulder and answered, "Yes." I fell on my knees before Him. Then slowly I raised my head and looked into His beautiful eyes and said, "I believe."

Hours later I set off for home. My errand could wait until another day. I had to go to Bethlehem, I had to find my brothers, I had to tell them, The King is in Jerusalem…

Healing Words

Alive again...

My children loved going to see any pantomime that was on stage around Christmas time; I must admit I was as excited as they were. Most pantomimes include at least one magician in a top hat and tails. With the theatre lights turned low and the spotlight on the stage, we would sit mesmerised at the illusions and tricks being performed. Even I wondered how someone could appear in an empty box and then disappear just as quickly!

After the show and a trip to the nearest chip shop, we would set off for home. The conversation in the car was always about the magic tricks, resulting in at least one or more of my children asking for a magic set from Santa. As adults we know that magic and illusions are not real, but try explaining this fact to excited children, who had seen a woman cut in half, it's not easy!

Martha, Mary and Lazarus loved Jesus and the three of them knew He could heal all manner of sickness. When Lazarus became ill, the sisters sent for Jesus. It was four days before He arrived in Bethany, by then it was too late, their brother was dead. The sisters were in despair. They believed in the healing power of Jesus, but they knew there was no way the death of their brother Lazarus could be reversed.

When Jesus asked Martha did she believe in Him, truly believe, she answered "yes!" Martha believed what she knew, but she did not understand what Jesus meant by His words, *"I am the resurrection and the life."* She believed that God would give life to everyone at the end of time.

When Lazarus appeared at the command of Jesus, the people of Bethany were amazed and thought it was an illusion or a trick. Later these same people along with Martha, Mary and their dear brother, praised God and rejoiced at the love Jesus had for each and every person in their little town.

Alive Again...

How happy we are, my dear brother, sweet sister and me
But things were different a short while ago,
There was heartache; there was sorrow, our tears overflowed
It happened this way...

Our brother took sick, a simple cold, Mary said
But doctors disagreed, shaking their heads,
"He's worse Martha, he'll be gone by morn"
My sister gave them a look of scorn,
"Oh no!" She said, "I've sent for our friend
I know He'll come before the night ends."

Our brother was dead by first morn light.
I covered the body keeping death from our sight,
Mary sobbed
 "Please, please keep him in the light
I know Jesus will come before dark of night."
We buried our brother at sunset.

Four days later I was still busy with guests
Mary couldn't help, I got no rest,
Then someone said, "The Master is here!"
I felt hurt in my heart, to my eyes came tears,
I hurried, wondering how to explain
Mary's absence, her grief, her unending pain.

Jesus sensed my distress; sadness came to His eyes
At all my questions beginning with why,
Then he asked, did I believe He was life, even in death?
I trusted our friend,
I had only one answer, "Yes Lord, yes"
I rushed back to Mary, "He wants you," I pressed.

She ran from the door, crying, "Master, why did you wait?"
"Our brother is dead, you came too late,"
Our Lord wasn't angry
But His face showed pain,
Then in front of us all
His tears fell like rain.

We went to the grave, the guests, Jesus, Mary and I
"Master" I said, "It's been four days,
Think of the body, the smell, the decay"
But he took no notice as he knelt down to pray,
The crowds went silent and stepped back in fear
When Jesus called out, "Lazarus, come here!"

My heart was thumping and beating so fast
Then from the crowds came fearful gasps,
Standing there
Was the brother we loved,
Alive again… back from the dead
Back from the grave.

There was great joy that day in Bethany town
But some day,
A greater joy will abound
Till then,
We trust and believe what our dear Saviour said,
"Yet shall ye live even though ye be dead."

Bartimaeus...

When my children were teenagers there was a daily ritual, perhaps you had the same routine in your home - in from school and straight into the grocery cupboard!

Each Friday morning I'd do a big shop, so big that by the time everything was packed away the cupboard shelves were groaning, needless to say the shelves stopped groaning by the following Tuesday.

The grocer would greet me on a Tuesday morning with the words, *'Empty again?'* I smiled as I placed tins of beans and cornflakes in my basket and repeated his words, *'Empty again.'*

As I returned to the car, the one apple that lay in the fruit bowl came to mind. I was about to return to the grocers, when I remembered we were going to visit my grandmother on Saturday. I could do my shopping in my home town, "groceries are groceries regardless of where you buy them" I thought as I packed the *'get me through to Saturday'* items in the car boot.

We arrived at my grandmother's little white-washed home at lunchtime. She had moved from the townhouse to the quietness of the countryside ten years ago. Her home had no electricity or water supply. She used to say, "A Tilly lamp sheds good light and spring water tastes better than piped!"

After lunch I was ready to face the Saturday crowds in the supermarket. "Go to the market for your fruit," my grandmother shouted, as I eased the car from the front door...Biddy the duck was arriving for her lunch of mushed-up bread and water.

It was late in the afternoon when I arrived at the market. Most of the stallholders were packing up their goods, but one was still serving customers. I picked up bananas and oranges, the one fruit I wanted was not priced. "What price are the apples?" I asked. The traders answer surprised me; "Two for the price of one." I bought six and got six free!

Later that night my daily Bible reading was in Mark 10:46-52. It was the story of Bartimaeus, an old blind man, a man the townsfolk had no time for, he was a nuisance, a beggar, a nobody.

If you have a moment let Bartimaeus '*the nobody*,' tell you about the day he met Jesus and received two gifts instead of one - his sight and Eternal life.

Bartimaeus...

Slowly I felt my way that day
Along the road to the old doorway,
My clothes were tattered, torn and old
But they shielded me from the morning cold.

As I sat within the frame of a door
By passing public was ignored,
I was just a pitiful soul
An old blind man with a begging bowl…

I felt so weary, I felt so cursed
I sat there not by choice,
But from the doorway I heard all
Tales of joy and some of gall…

That day I heard some different news
A healing man who asked no dues,
A Nazarene, Jericho-bound
Was passing through our busy town…

They said, He made a cripple stand
And hearing brought to born deaf man,
As someone said, "He's in the street"
I left my wooden doorway seat…

Bartimaeus...

I listened to feet upon the ground
Sensed crowds of people milling around,
"Sir" I shouted, "Sir
Please let a blind man see..."

Then I felt fear, He stood so near
And when He spoke His voice was clear,
"What do you want?" He asked of me
"Please," I said, "Please let Bartimaeus see."

Again He spoke and my heart raced
So close His breath upon my face,
Then came my tears, I saw daylight
I saw the face that gave me sight.

All those who stood around
Saw me kneel upon the ground,
With eyes now open to His light
My heart received His Love and Gift of Life.

Reaching out...

All children go through the stage of the wants. I recall a visit to a toy store in the company of my youngest son - bad idea. We were shopping for a gift for my daughter's birthday. As soon as we walked through the door, he disappeared like a rabbit down a hole. Minutes later he returned with one of the most expensive toy cars in the shop. No amount of explaining would convince him it was his sister's birthday and we were shopping for her. His lip dropped as I placed the car back on the shelf. Even the promise of ice-cream didn't work! By now his tears were flowing and we were starting to attract a few raised eyebrows. Finally, he agreed to accept my bribe of toy cowboys and Indians. "Problem solved," I thought, but no, he then said we needed gifts for his two brothers! As we left the shop, with more than I had intended to buy, his sad eyes looked again at the expensive toy car, "Christmas is coming," I said. His smile returned...

One woman we read of in the Bible was not so easily put off. She was told of a preacher named Jesus, who could heal sickness, and she wondered if He would heal her. She wanted to be healed and was determined and adamant to be healed at all costs. Jesus was her last hope.

She pushed and shoved until she was almost within reach of finding help. The crowd pushed against her, but she couldn't get through, she couldn't see Jesus. In desperation, she knelt down and struggled against the crowd. She reached out her hand and within moments, her determination and faith allowed her to grasp the hem of His cloak.

Unlike this woman, we don't need to push through the crowds to touch Jesus, He is close to us when we reach out in prayer. If you have a moment, let this sick woman tell you about that day Jesus came to her town…

Reaching Out...

The knock on the door was loud and clear, crossly I shouted,
"Come in!"
It was a friend, just one of few, who daily came to cook and clean,
I should have been thankful, showed some cheer
 But I'd become bad tempered with the passing years,
My moaning and groaning kept neighbours at bay
My spirit was broken, I couldn't even pray.

My friend was excited as she sat down
She said, "the healer Jesus is passing through town,
And in a village the other day
He helped a man, his first words to say,
And a man born blind could see today
When Jesus placed on his eyes some clay."

My friend left and I was alone
If I could just see this Jesus, again I moaned,
For twelve long years I'd been unwell
My money all gone, nothing left to sell,
I'd paid doctors from far and near
But not one ever found me a cure.

In pain I dressed, my body like wood
I had to hurry, oh if only I could,
The door was ajar because of the heat
To my ears came the sound of running feet,
As I struggled, hot tears filled my eye
I had to hurry or he'd pass me by.

I prayed "Please help me God"
I need to see Jesus the healer today,"
When I reached the road I was in distress
The people were pushing and against me pressed,
I couldn't see Jesus…
Then someone moved in the crowd and I found a space.

But Jesus had almost passed by
I saw His cloak, His sandaled feet,
I put out my hand, "Please God, just let me reach
If I can just touch the hem of His cloak, one touch…,"
Then as my hand on the hem of His cloak was laid
I trembled in fear from my feet to my head

In that instant, my sickness and pain was relieved
I believed Jesus could help, but how I knew not,
It seemed His healing power came straight through the cloth
My joy was short-lived as I heard Him say,
"Who has been healed,
Who has touched me today?"

But Jesus knew, though I made no sound
He turned from the crowd, and looked down,
And found me crouched low on the ground
I was afraid; I had broken the ban,
I had defied the law
By touching a man… with my unclean hand.

I wanted to beg His forgiveness
I wanted to flee,
But before I could speak, He spoke to me
So gently He said,
"Woman, go on your way…
your faith in me has healed you today."

Life water...

My first encounter with television was in 1953, the programme being televised was the Queen's Coronation. All children had a day off school for the occasion, but not all children had the opportunity of seeing the Queen in all her finery.

I, with family members, strained our eyes to see the happenings on a 14-inch screen. The TV had squiggly lines and the live pictures came to us in black and white. To a thirteen-year-old girl, the idea of something happening hundreds of miles away and being able to see it as it happened, was magic.

Today when the original coronation footage is shown, it appears as it did that day in London, in glorious colour. Every time I see a repeat, I think back to the squiggly lines and my screwed-up eyes.

By 1964, my husband and I had finally saved enough money for a deposit in order to rent a magic box. The addition of a TV brought changes to our household. There were programmes to watch instead of going for a walk, the dinner had to be served before the six o'clock news and my books became redundant.

As the years passed, adverts made their appearance on certain channels. We were and still are reminded of the things we need to make us happy. We are guaranteed to be loved by the people in our life, if we use a particular brand of shampoo or launder our clothes with a certain washing power. Sometimes I'd smile when I think of the big red bars of Lifebuoy soap we used as children on our hair and everywhere else, not to mention the bars of Sunlight soap that was used by all housewives on washday.

The many adverts that confront us each week made me think about a Biblical woman, she was under pressure of a different type.

What she was thinking about that day? She had had men in her life but they never seemed to stay long. Perhaps she was wondering how to keep the present man she was living with. What unhappy thoughts were in her heart the day she went to fetch a bucket of water. The woman wanted to love and be loved, but inwardly she felt guilty, perhaps she had never admitted the truth to herself, until that day.

Admitting the truth to ourselves is the hardest truth of all.

Life Water...

I was unhappy that day, unhappy with life
I had so many thoughts, so much strife, what more could I do?
I could buy a new cloak, but what colour,
ruby red or perhaps palest blue
New beads and a bottle of perfume,
perhaps then my dream would come true.

I wanted to be happily married,
and have feelings of great pride and joy
With children loving and tender, a sweet girl and a dear little boy,
To be able to go to the market and hold my head up high
To say, 'Good morning' to neighbours,
instead of hiding as they pass by.

Every day I went to fetch water, alone I went to the well
Avoiding the village women with their titters and stories to tell,
They never felt my hurt, they never felt my shame
Nor did they feel any pity,
when they spat or called me foul names.

That day as I drew of the water, I was surprised by the voice of a man
I turned at the words of the stranger
and He knew by my unsettled calm,
He knew from the look on my face,
that He didn't belong in Samaria
Jews never would visit this place.

He carried no rope or bucket not even a jar was in sight
When He asked for a drink I gave, to me it only seemed right,
He drank then paused to inquire,
"Who is the man in your house?"
I answered; then wanted to hide, or flee like a little grey mouse.

"I know," He said. "I know he's the last one of five"
How did this strange man guess and why did I tell Him no lies,
I thought Him to be a prophet, for only a prophet could see
A woman that was so lonely and a heart that longed to be free.

Our talk then turned to Messiah
I said, "We are waiting for Him,"
This stranger turned to me gently, this lone man without kith or kin
"Mam" He said, "Mam you are talking to Him."

That day I ran for the town folk, I begged and pleaded, "Please come
Come and meet the Messiah, He's here, the Saviour, God's Son,"
The people all rushed to greet Him, asking for freedom from sin
Jesus blessed and forgave us and that day we rejoiced with Him.

As once more I retell my story, of that day at old Jacob's well
I pray you will hear my message and on it your thoughts will dwell,
And just as I searched, are you searching for freedom within
If you are, come drink from the cup that Christ offers, filled with
love from His life-giving spring…

Changed ways...

I opened my eyes in time to switch off the alarm clock, I didn't need the buzzer to remind me that it was the start of another humdrum day.

The morning ritual had already started as I entered the kitchen; "Mum, I can't find my P.E. pants?" "Mum did you lift my book?" Every morning without fail, one or more of my children, had lost or misplaced something! The lost something's were usually found beneath their beds!

An hour later, I closed the front door and went into the kitchen. I stood for a few minutes and listened to the silence. The quietness was approved by Tom the cat as he lay curled up on one of my cardigans. "Peace and quietness is the only way to start the day," I said to the sleeping cat, as I poured myself another cup of tea.

By 11am the house was ship-shape and another job was on the horizon, the garden with its flourishing weeds! Then the phone rang.

I walked into the kitchen and did a war dance around the table! The cat let out a screech and the budgie flapped his wings like an eagle! I put the kettle on. It was time to think.

My mother-in-law had rang to say she would visit about four o'clock that afternoon. I loved her and loved to visit her spotless home. She was a great pastry cook, her fairy cakes always had smooth tops, unlike mine, that looked, and at times, tasted like the Rocky Mountains on a bad day!

In all my married life I had never known Mrs H senior to get in a tizzy. She used to say, "When things go wrong, say a little prayer and make time for Jesus." Advice that I kept in my heart and still keep, although there are times, when things go every which way, that I still do a war dance!

We had a great afternoon and my fairy cakes were perfect! As I kissed my mother-in-law goodbye that evening, I was thankful for a dear, kind woman who loved God with all her heart.

I know of another woman; who got in a tizzy, her name was Martha. She was always busy, but unlike me, she didn't have the help of a washing machine, electric cooker or water on tap. Come into her home and meet her, she's waiting…

Changed Ways...

It was one of those mornings, you know the sort I mean
When you look around the house
And just everything needs cleaned,
I had risen early, many chores were needing done
In the coolness of the morning; before the noonday sun…

I was busy with the wash and faraway in thought
When my brother dashed in, I almost dropped the pot!
"Martha" he said, "the Master's coming and His trusted friends
Dearest Martha,
Will you cook some dinner, for these travel-weary men?"

Rudely I shouted, "Where will I get the hands?
I have to finish the wash I have to sweep the rooms,
I have to bake the bread; by then it will be noon,
"Why can't you ask Mary to help prepare the food?
And she can do the cooking, her meals taste just as good."

"Now be off with you!" I told him "before my temper breaks
It's always Martha do this or Martha go fetch,
Oh yes, our sister will be here, if it's to sing, or play a merry tune
But never is she here when chores are needing done,
It's me, good old Martha, who works her fingers to the bone."

My brother left looking sad
Why was I so cross with a brother sweet and dear?
 It's my own fault, sure I'm always first to volunteer
Let me see now, there's Jesus, His disciples, Lazarus, Mary and me
That makes sixteen for dinner, oh dear, oh deary deary me.

I rushed and rushed and soon it was all done
The washing, cooking, cleaning, just before the midday sun,
I was in the kitchen when the visitors arrived
A soft voice called out, "Martha, come sit by me a while,
And don't be cross with Mary…, now, let me see your smile. "

I'm old Martha now, still happy in my home
Doing all the things I do but without the moans,
The Master's words that day made me understand
The love of God within my life means more,
Than cooking, or cleaning pots and pans.

Yes, I listened to the Master and He calls to you today
Be it in the kitchen, the workplace or at play,
He waits on you to come and sit by Him a while
He calls and waits for you,
His precious much-loved child.

Empty nets...

Most of the disciples were born into the fishing community and took on the profession of their fathers and grandfathers. When they became followers of Jesus they still used their fishing skills for food. Being able to handle a boat allowed them to cross the sea to another part of their country instead of walking for days. The disciples were at Jesus' side most of the time and had witnessed many miracles, but they were still apprentices and in training. They loved and trusted Jesus, until that day on the Sea of Galilee.

Everything was fine when they set sail. They were kept busy tending to nets and sails, perhaps their thoughts were on home, dinner and bed. All thoughts left them when a sudden storm arose and almost capsized the boat. They were so scared they even forgot that Jesus was asleep. When someone did remember, it made the panic worse. The fear of everyone drowning blotted out everything Jesus had taught them about trust and faith in Him. But then Jesus calmed the sea, and not only did the storm disappear but also their anxiety.

This Bible story speaks to all of us. As Christians we know God is with us at all times, yet like the disciples we often forget. Faith and trust gets set aside when everything is well in our world. Panic sets in when things go every-which-way. That's when fear grabs us and holds on tight. We try to put things right but many times to no avail. Shame-faced we turn to God in prayer. God understands our humanity. He touches our heart with His love, He dispels all fear and calms our hearts. A heart that is stilled and filled with His love is a heart that can contend with anything that befalls use.

We don't have first-hand experience of the wondrous workings that Jesus did in the company of the fishermen. What we do have is the power of prayer that comes from trusting and believing the one true God and His son Jesus. A loving God who is an ever-present help in times of trouble.

Empty Nets...

It had been a long hard day, we were all tired out
Home and bed sounded good, there was no doubt,
But then, the Master said,
"Cross over the water, it's just six short miles"
He looked so weary, I couldn't decline,
As I gave the order His smile met mine.

When we cast off, I saw the Master lie down
I hoped He would sleep,
He looked like a child, not a line on his face,
Content to be here
Always content, regardless of place.

As the breeze carried us far from the shore,
I glimpsed in the distance
Twinkling lights, lights that said families were home for the night,
We were three miles out, when the wind rose with a roar
I didn't worry, I'd seen these squalls before,
But I was proved wrong, when waves washed the deck floor.

Many times I'd seen the weather turn rough...
We were trying our best to ride out the storm,
When someone shouted, "Wake the Master!"
I'd been so busy, tying sails, fixing ropes,
I'd forgotten about Jesus in the stern of the boat.

Can you imagine our fear and confusion
As winds howled and screamed like angry demons,
And the next thing that happened, caused us to fear
There stood the Master, His words, "Be quiet, be still,"
Made the elements obey and come under His will.

As He turned to us, did He read our thoughts?
I knew that some of us drew the conclusion,
That He had performed some sort of illusion
We all felt shame when He said, "Where is your faith?"
We should have known, with Him we were safe.

 We stood in silence…
With the sea now calm and no wind for our sail,
We had time to think of how we had failed
Our lack of faith brought sadness that day,
From then on, we vowed to trust and obey.

Yes…
We had so much to learn,
So much to learn from our Master and friend
Our Lord and Master,
Who called us to be… Fishers of Men

Peace...

I was a very inquisitive and possibly, irritating child when I was at school. The words *'why, what, when, how'* seemed to be forever in my mouth, especially in history class. I wanted to know more about the subject than the class time allowed. One morning my questions had interrupted the teacher three times. He walked to the middle of the room and yelled very loudly, "Give my head peace!" Those words were like a red rag to a bull as my hand shot up; "Sir," I asked, "is your head at war?" His answer was unrepeatable as it came through tight, clenched teeth! I spent the next ten minutes outside the classroom door with ruler marks printed on my palm!

The Pharisees in the Bible were forever questioning Jesus, "Teacher, we want to see a sign from you". Is it lawful to give a poll-tax to Caesar or not?" "Is it lawful to heal on the Sabbath?" Jesus answered all their questions and sometimes He answered with a question.

After these times of questions and trickery, I like to think of Jesus going somewhere far away from the crowds of unbelieving religious leaders. One place He loved was the Sea of Galilee; perhaps He walked on that tranquil beach quite often.

Peace…

Pink clouds that lingered in the west
Now guide the golden sun to rest,
On tiptoe comes a pale grey sky
To kiss the blue of day goodbye.

Lazy waves with white edged crest
On empty beach now come to rest,
Overhead a lone gull cries
As tranquil sea whispers and sighs.

Dunes of flaxen, sleeping sand
Curve and lean against the land,
A baby crab unhurried creeps
From ocean play to welcome sleep.

Soft starlight in the velvet night
Pale moon that casts its silver light,
Past memories at last released
The heart is quiet… all is peace.

Voices around the Cross...

The Old Misfit...

I was almost seven years old when the great winter snow of 1946-47 came falling from the sky. The snow fluttered down like soft white feathers. Within hours, the fluttering feathers seemed to join together to form a thick blanket, making it impossible to see the other side of the street! I was delighted, as were my friends. The snow continued all that day and night; little did we know some of it would still be laying in grubby heaps until Easter!

Playing in snow was great fun until your fingers and toes started to nip, when that happened we headed for whoever's home was the nearest. Wet everything's were replaced with dry everything's and we would sit toasting ourselves at a fire piled high with coal and odd-shaped blocks.

The burning wood fascinated me, some of it spat bright sparks onto the hearth, some hissed like snakes and some had purple flames. All the families in our street had stockpiles of wood, as the saw-mill was just ten minutes from where we lived. Some blocks were free of charge, this wood came from ancient twisted trees and had no value to the mill owner. Occasionally, planks would be returned from factories, these were named misfits due to being cut too thick or having too many knots. Twisted, smooth or knotty, the wood did the same thing, it thawed out frozen fingers and toes. 1946-47 was a year of hardship for many people across the U.K. As children, we never worried about grown up things, we were too busy building snowmen.

Many times over the years I've thought about the crucifixion tree.

The well-known Easter hymn, 'The Old Rugged Cross,' speaks to me of a tree that was well weathered but had survived. Perhaps the cross was cut from such a tree, a tree that had no value, a misfit that shared its forest home alongside flawless ones.

An old gnarled tree that two-thousand years later is still remembered by Christians worldwide. A tree that tells of the great love God had for each one of us, a love so great that He sacrificed His only Son for our sins.

The cross of Christ speaks silently to us all, 'on me The King of Glory died, that you may live again.'

The Old Misfit...

I was just a woodsman; I seldom came to town
I cared for the trees from sunrise till sundown,
Sometimes I'd sit a-dreaming, when my day's work was done
Thinking of my trees in the hands of man and son,
I could see chairs and tables, ladders and strong gates
Yes, my trees were first class and earned me good rates...

But, deep in the forest there grew one old tree
Aged, bent and gnarled, a little bit like me,
When I sat beneath it, peace of mind I'd find
An old man and a tree, both well past our prime,
I always felt contented as against it I leaned
Admiring all the other trees, in coats of brightest green...

I lived in peace, until the soldiers came
Looking for a tree, one that would shame,
They searched from early morn, then in the fading light
Their laughter told me, my tree was in their sight,
"Here it is," they cried, "this is the very one
It will suit the liar, who claims to be God's Son..."

Harshly they bound what they called '*The Old Misfit*'
The taut rope leaving cuts as deep as any whip,
Next day, I had to travel with my tree of many years
To the dreaded place, the shameful place, I call the hill of tears,
I saw the man, I knew his face
I turned away as iron pierced…

Slowly, the tree was raised in view of town and land
I saw His head, His feet, His hands,
Some people jeered as others prayed
I looked again, then crept away,
I knew the man, a preaching man, a man of Jewish race
What did he do, what law offend, to die in such disgrace…

That night…
The old tree stood in blood-stained mire,
Waiting for its one last fate, the cleansing flame of fire
But men came asking,
And before the light of day
 I went with them; we eased it down, and carried it away…

Once long ago an old tree stood in a forest dark
Today it stands in bright light, gone now its deathly mark,
And each time you see it, carved in silver, wood or gold
Let it tell the story,
Of how 2000 years ago
Jesus the Christ was crucified, because He loved you so…

The Soldier...

Have you ever agreed to be on a committee? Unfortunately at the time of agreement, you didn't realise that one person and one person only would make all the rules and decisions, the chairperson. Sometimes you may not have been in agreement with items on the agenda, but your ideas or suggestions fall on deaf ears. You can only accept the fact, you signed your name on the form and it's your duty to abide by the head of the committee.

In the Bible we read of people having to comply. One being King Herod Antipas, he had pledged his stepdaughter Salome anything she wanted, if she danced for him. She asked for the head of John the Baptist. The king could not break his word; he had to fulfil his promise.

Joining the Roman Guard meant signing up for unspecified duties. The enlisted men had to enforce the law of the land and had no choice of where they would be based.

At our Lord's crucifixion, one soldier was ordered to end Christ's life, he had no choice; to have refused would have meant imprisonment or death. A second before he carried out the final deed he was just another soldier. As the spear punctured our Lord's side, something happened, a realisation; the soldier's words, *"Truly this man is the Son of God."*

His words convince me, that his days as a soldier were over and his life was changed for ever.,,

The Soldier...

"Draw your spear, pierce his side
Make sure the Nazarene has died,"
Orders from my superior came
I held back, feeling shame…

Then gripping tight my blade of steel
I obeyed this last ordeal,
As blood gushed like bright red wine
Anxious thoughts flashed to mind…

This man born of Jewish race
Crucified in deep disgrace,
Slowly he dies on a wretched tree
As a guilty one swiftly flees…

Strong feelings of my soldier pride
Bring confusion deep inside,
From Roman law that does abide
My glory thoughts are now denied…

As darkness falls upon the land
I'll cast my blade from trembling hand,
Somehow I know it's my last day
To draw a sword for a soldier pay…

The words of this poor dying man
I need great help to understand,
Peace of mind I need this day
For deeds and orders I obeyed.

Soon this hour will pass away
The dead removed without delay,
And then will come the dark of night
When I'll seek answers to my plight…

I'll search for all the fishermen
And the woman, Magdalene,
Till then I stand with blood-stained hands
A soldier… weeping for a preaching man…

Freedom day…

Hot tired feet and swollen ankles were the result of a day's shopping. My front door never looked so good as I staggered through it. Without even putting my packages away, I kicked off my fashionable high-heeled shoes. I could almost hear my feet shout out *"freedom!"* The shoes were retired to the back of a cupboard and only worn on special occasions!

Liberation comes in many shapes and forms, I recall two good friends and I going to the indoor swimming pool for the first time. They chose a time when the pool would be almost empty, I didn't mind how many swimmers would be there, but they were insistent. My friends were very conscious of their figure. There was never a bump or a fold, just smoothness in their close-fitting clothes, until that afternoon. The lycra swimsuits gave their bodies complete freedom for an hour! Gone were the in-pulling undergarments, or as my friends call them, corsets and stays.

An hour later, in the changing room, the bumps and folds had disappeared. Tight fitting undergarments can conceal a mountain of cream buns consumed at church gatherings. But then, a polite, '*no thank you*.' is hard to say when a member of the tea committee says, "Oh go on, I made them especially for tonight."

There are many types of freedom. Freedom to worship in our churches or chapels is something we here in the West take for granted. The media brings news, sometimes on a daily basis, of churches burned down and preachers killed or maimed. In the busyness of our life we sometimes forget.

The Easter story tells us of another freedom. On Good Friday morning, Barabbas was given his liberty. He was pardoned. I'm sure he struggled to understand his judges and their reasoning. He knew he was guilty but he wasn't about to argue the point. He kept his thoughts hidden and shrugged off all that had happened that morning. Or did he? The day Christ was crucified was supposed to be the freedom day for Barabbas, but was it? What were his thoughts? Did he watch the gruelling scene as his two friends and a preacher man slowly died?

In my poem I have tried to see into the heart of a man, a man who knew it was not his freedom day - but his first day in a life sentence of guilt.

Freedom Day...

I stand within a rowdy crowd
Feeling anything but proud,
A man is dying, one of three
I am pardoned, I am free…

Their reason I can't understand
To crucify a preacher man,
Yet, I am glad to breathe the air
In exchange for blood-soaked hair…

I am a thief, a man of greed
Yet, I never had to plead,
Freed, because the people said
'We don't want Barabbas dead…'

Freedom Day...

I stand here by choice of will
Instead of fleeing from this hill,
Listening as the preacher speaks
Seeing tears my comrades weep…

Three men on crosses on a hill
Nailed and beaten, hanging still,
On the preacher's head a crown
Above it, 'King of Jews' is found…'

I stand here confused inside
Alive and free, death denied,
A Nazarene takes all the blame
And dies upon the cross of shame…

Glints of sun on a blood-stained blade
At last the preacher's pain can fade,
I bow my head, I creep away
On what is called… My Freedom Day…

The Donkey's Tale...

When I was a little girl I loved to daydream. I could imagine my long blonde hair, beautiful gowns and shiny silvery shoes. My home was a castle; I had three dogs, two ponies and an endless supply of sweets!

I've lost count of the many times the gentle voice of my Grandmother had me leave my castle and return back to reality and the real me. My hair was black and hung in what is best described as rat tails, I had a squint in my left eye, my clothes were home-made and my shoes were always the same colour, plain brown! Is it any wonder I daydreamed?

I remember one day when I was six years old and sitting in my primary two classroom doing what I loved to do best, daydream. Although Christmas was six months away, I hoped Santa would bring me a pair of roller skates with red leather laces.

My teacher, unknown to me had been talking about our new reading book. She was asking questions and then pointed at me and asked, "What colour was Peter's hat?" I was still in my dreamy state; didn't hear the question properly and answered, "Any colour of laces." Without taking a breath my teacher yelled, "You are a stupid donkey!" Everyone laughed. I wanted to shout, 'Donkeys aren't stupid, if they were, Mary would have had to walk all the way to Bethlehem!'

Days after my humiliation I scribbled down a few words about donkeys and Christmas. The note was forgotten until a few years after I left school. I was clearing out boxes and there, yellow and faded, was my donkey note. I looked at it and decided that someday I would write about the donkey in the Christmas story.

Years later sitting at my typewriter, the note now the worse for wear, was peeking out from a pile of other notes. I recall my own words, "Little donkey, please talk to me." Now I, like everyone else, know that donkeys can't talk, but a strange thing happened, the words of the poem **'The Donkeys Tale'** came to my mind. Then other thoughts came, perhaps that same little donkey was in Jerusalem on Good Friday.

The Donkey's Tale…

If you have a moment, come and meet my special donkey, a donkey that has been in my thoughts for seventy plus years, and first met the light of day in 1969…

The Donkey's Tale…

Many years have passed since that winters night
When we were all alone, the stars our only light,
On and on I plodded,
Until the straight road took a bend,
And then at last I saw, the glow of Bethlehem.

Door on door my master knocked, I knew we were too late
But slowly I followed till we reached a byre gate,
It was there I heard his pleadings and then another say
"Come use the stable; let the woman rest awhile,"
I shook my tail and thought, 'a stable, to birth a First-born Child.'

I watched as my master shaped a bed from clean-cut hay
And soon upon a homespun rug, the Child and mother lay,
I looked on proudly and the master's words recalled
"The Baby to be born, will be special all His days,
He will be a Saviour and men will change their ways…"

I stood in the corner near the cattle and the sheep
I had to tell them crossly,
"Do be quiet, can't you see, the special Child's asleep"
I was about to tell them, I was special too,
For I had information, no creature or other donkey knew.

But I was interrupted, when from the stable door,
I heard voices, there were two or three, or maybe it was four,
"We've come to see the Baby, to worship and adore."
From my corner I could see,
A crowd of shepherd men, kneeling on the floor.

I watched those men's faces and the glow that spread around,
These men were so happy, it seemed a treasure they had found,
Yet, there was no laughter, not a single sound
I glanced again at the little One asleep in the manger stall,
Once more I thought of the master's words, "A Saviour for us all."

Yes, I remember, more than thirty years ago
I still can see the stable, the shepherds and the star,
The precious gifts from wise men that travelled from afar,
And I can see the Man-child, asleep in a manger bed
Yes, I remember that holy night and what the master said.

Today, I stand and watch the gentle mother watch her Son,
Silently she stands, as death throes slowly come,
Is she remembering that first time, a time so long ago
When she kissed His tiny head and said, "My Son I love you so."
Yes, she is remembering… her quiet tears tell me so.

I am just a donkey, growing old with passing time,
An old donkey who remembers,
 The gift God gave to men
That night so long ago, in a town called Bethlehem.

Memories

Evening shadows...

When my friends and I were children we were privileged to have three princesses, a racing driver, and a doctor visit our street on a weekly visit. Sometimes the princesses were busy and shopkeepers came in their place. Depending on the weather, the professional men would send cowboys as stand-ins. Dressed in beautiful clothes and jewels, the princesses would watch as cows were rounded up or a racing car was washed and polished.

When the call, *"dinners ready"* came from one or more of the small white-washed houses, the cows and finery would disappear.

Once again plain Janes and Johns left their cardboard boxes, torn sheets, tin buckets, and broken glass - the world of make-believe could start again another day.

As the years passed and we emerged into adulthood, our fantasy world ended. Each of us eventually married and had children of our own, none of us ever became princesses or cowboys!

All children, no matter what era they are born into, play at make-believe. I know of a woman who lived more than two-thousand years ago and I've often wondered if she played imaginary games when she was a little girl. She was a privileged child and came from a very respectable and financially secure home. Unfortunately as she grew into her adult years, she was plagued with various health issues. She was always anxious and had bouts of anger, so much so that people believed she was full of devilish wickedness.

As time passed, her malady became worse and she left her family home. Some people say she took to wandering the streets at night. This young woman, who had a happy home life and never wanted for anything, now had to beg for food. As a child, if she did play the imaginary game of who she might someday be, I'm sure she never thought she would end up living an impoverished and degrading existence.

The woman was Mary Magdalene, one night as she walked the lonely dim-lit streets she met Jesus. At that first encounter Jesus saw a woman with no peace of mind or control of will. He looked on her with compassionate eyes, eyes that saw into her hurting soul. That night Jesus, in His loving mercy, healed Mary of all her afflictions, and in doing so, changed her life forever.

As she stood on Golgotha's hill, her heartache and memories must have been overwhelming.

Evening Shadows...

Alone I stand on a windswept hill
Weeping bitter tears at will,
Memories stir, aroused they speak
Of a sour life mixed with sweet.

Men of grandeur my favours sought
Their silver coin my pleasure bought,
My dreams of finery and sweet wine,
Concealed the truth, I was blind.

My rich companions didn't last
The easy money dwindled fast,
I had reached hells blackest gate,
With decadent men to share my fate.

Years of high life took their toll
My heart so young, my body old,
With tired eyes I walked the town
A haggard face in a tattered gown.

Then, that night I stood alone
Shadowed streets my lowly home,
My clothes and hair so dirt ingrained,
Yet in my heart, I felt no shame.

The stranger almost passed me by
As I stepped out in hunger's ply,
When I tried to offer Him my wares
His words, His eyes, laid my soul bare.

New life, new hope, He offered me
He said that I, I could be free,
Free to walk from that hellish place
Free to live a life of grace.

My tears fall on the blood-stained ground
Gone now the life, the love, I found,
I stand and weep in death's cold chill
Alone I stand, on a windswept hill.

Broken friendship...

The media often reports of innocent people being imprisoned. Those about to be incarcerated try to prove their innocence in a court of law and it is difficult when no one comes to their defence. A prisoner may plead and beg those who know he is guiltless to come forward. Many times important evidence is withheld by those who could help, but turn a deaf ear. Perhaps witnesses have small niggling doubts, are frightened of reprisals or they may hold a long-standing grudge against the accused. In most cases, the penalty of imprisonment is carried out. Sometimes a witness may have a guilty conscience and will come forward. In the case of the death penalty, it is often too late.

The trial and death of Jesus was the greatest miscarriage of justice to ever have happened. Hundreds of people knew He was innocent, yet not one gave evidence in His favour. Jesus stood alone. His disciples, who knew Him intimately for three years, turned their backs. Peter, the one disciple who could have been a witness, denied knowing Jesus, not once but three times.

Peter was human; the fear of the atrocities carried out by the Roman guard pushed all thoughts of loyalty, love and friendship from his mind. The intrinsic power of survival took over and blocked out the consequences of his answer. We all could feel anger at Peter's response, but if you or I had stood in the High Priest's courtyard, would we have answered anything different? Today, many Christians keep their faith to themselves out of embarrassment, fear of losing friends, or conflict in the family. All these and more make us as guilty as the disciple Peter.

With every blow of the hammer, with every pierce of the thorn, Peter knew he had aided in the torture and suffering of his loving Master and Friend. In his guilty heart, he knew he would live the rest of his life in deep regret.

Unknown to Peter, God had other plans...

Broken Friendship...

Yesterday I had my friend
Happy to follow where and when,
We dallied slowly through the pass
Unknown to me it would be our last.

Why was I so deaf and blind
To games another had in mind?
I never knew of secret plans
Or silver in a traitor's hand.

The kiss given in pretence
His trial held but no defence,
A mocking robe, a thorny crown
Sneers and jibes from all around.

To questions asked, three times I lied
I should have stood there by his side,
I should have said; 'Yes, he is my friend
And I Peter, His life defend.'

The walk to Golgotha's hill
Nails used with expert skill,
His mother's sobs amid the jeers
Her heartache showing in her tears.

The greediness of swarming flies
In bloodied hair and red rimmed eyes,
Chest heaving with each breath
All around the smell of death.

Winds howling over the land
As spirit leaves this holy man,
A soldier casting blade to sand
Knew this death was underhand.

Gone from me my dearest friend
Judged and killed by evil men
I pray for those so hatred bound,
And mercy on Jerusalem town.

I linger at His grave,
Alone with my shame,
Lies etched deep on my heart
My friend is dead… I am to blame.

A sleepless night…

Like all children, I had sleepless nights, some of these nights happened as I waited for Christmas morning. Thoughts of the toys I had asked for, along with the anticipation of my Grandmother's yearly fruit pudding, jiggled with counting the proverbial sheep.

I used to wonder why the pudding only appeared at Christmas time, years later I understood why. If we had food rationing today, as in the years from 1939 to 1946, we would be excited about a simple fruit pudding!

Perhaps some of you will remember the days of ration books and clothing coupons, or have listened as parents or grandparents talked about those years of neediness.

Most of my restless nights were forgotten the following day, but some of the night-thoughts that came with my tossing and turning stayed with me for days. One of my main concerns at ten years old was transferring from primary school to the *big* school. By 3pm however, on my first day at the Secondary Model School, I knew that my worrying had been pointless.

Years later when I was blessed with motherhood, sleepless nights were well and truly a part of my life, it seemed as if a note came with each child saying, 'worry included.'

I know you will agree with me when I say, worrying is best done during daylight hours, but no, it seems we have an in-built trait in our brain that wakes up the minute our heads hit the pillow! Worrying about job prospects, concern over the health of a loved one, even what to cook on Sunday when your in-laws come to lunch!

I know of a man and I think he had more than a few sleepless nights. His name was Nicodemus. Although he was educated and held a high position in the Jerusalem synagogue, he kept an open mind on all the happenings in the city, especially where prophet's and holy men were concerned.

When he heard about Jesus, he just had to find out more. His curiosity led him to the truth. I'm sure Nicodemus didn't sleep much on crucifixion night. Over the years I've often wondered what his thoughts were in the quietness of his home…

A Sleepless Night...

We used the spices I had brought
Then wrapped the Preacher in linen cloth,
We had no words to say
In the quietness of death, we turned and walked away.

As I sit here in my home
I relive again... the last few hours...,
The blood, the nails, his torn side
His forgiving words before He died.

I'd listened to the Preacher many times
At the back of the crowd I'd stand,
So many questions I would have asked,
But how could I?

I, who held position in the land
I could not, dare not, let the people see,
That I would talk with a Preaching Man
A man from Galilee.

And yet, I remember that night
I wrapped my cloak around me tight,
I wanted to talk with the Nazarene
In the darkness, I hoped I wouldn't be seen.

I stood in the shadows
I waited till the crowd dispersed,
Then slowly I approached the Man
Who spoke of love and peace on earth.

I had so many questions, one came to mind
"Teacher, how can I be born again?"
Before He spoke, His eyes searched mine,
What did He see, this Man from Galilee?

"Oh Nicodemus, you who teach other Jews
If you trust, believe I am Gods Son,
Understanding will descend
Then, as a new born child, you will live again."

All these thoughts, my mind is tired
Sleep I know won't come,
I linger with the preacher man
His words that night… His eyes searching mine.

And Joseph words, "How could they crucify my Lord?"
The darkness fades, morning light creeps in,
What will it bring, for a Pharisee
Who opposed His death, defied and felt the sting.

One who is unsure
One who helped lay him in a borrowed tomb,
A man Joseph called the `Saviour of all men`,
A Nazarene who said to me, "Ye must be born again."

Sweet wine...

Weddings could be described in two words, joyful and stressful. Joy can be clearly seen in the bride's eyes, smiles take up residence on the faces of the family and guests. Stress on the other hand, resides with the bride's mother, it lurks behind her calm smile, whispering, *'Did I remember, did I forget?'*

Thirty years ago, my daughter's wedding day was fast approaching and I was delegated to the job of chief organiser. There were times in-between being cook, laundry maid, telephonist and taxi driver that I often wished the clock would stop. Many times I retreated to my thinking space in the backyard, kitted out in an old raincoat and welly boots. Scrubbing the yard took away the thoughts of bridal flowers and wondering if the unfinished wedding cake would make it to the reception on time!

The wedding morning arrived and found me taking on the status of a mother hen with fidgety chicks! My three sons duly arrived downstairs looking like penguins in their top hats and tails. I was so glad they had taken my strong advice, "Yes, you must wear ties," I told them. My second son had a very flushed face. "Are you alright?" I asked, as I touched his forehead.

"Yes, Mum," he said; "I just need a cuppa." Ten minutes later I was in the kitchen searching for a safety pin, just in case an emergency cropped up, my rosy faced son was sipping his tea. The flush on his face had spread and he was straining his red neck upwards, just like a giraffe does when it plucks leaves from a tree. He pointed to his stretched neck. I examined his face and neck, then I asked with a stifled giggle, "Did you remove the cardboard from below the shirt collar?" His neck returned to normal!

At the end of the reception, the staff said they couldn't help but eavesdrop on some funny conversations, not to mention the hilarious jokes from the minister and the best man.

At home that night I mentally went over the events of the day. It was the comments of the serving staff about eavesdropping that had me thinking of another wedding. The wedding in Cana of Galilee. There would have been serving maids, it was possible that some of the groom's relations helped out at the tables. Perhaps one young maid saw Jesus perform the first miracle.

Sweet Wine…

I couldn't believe it when my friend said,
"The one you call Lord, has been crucified, He's dead…"

I'd been away on an errand and stayed overnight
I thought, my friend must be mistaken, she couldn't be right,
But next day word came to me
The Master is dead, hung from a tree.

It was just three years ago that the wedding took place
I was employed to serve food and help with the guests,
Jesus arrived with a woman and six other men
"Another priest," someone said, but to me, He looked very plain.

I was near the woman; I heard her say, "Son, the wine is all done"
His answer was lost in the din of the crowd,
But His next words were spoken so clear and loud,
"Fill the jars by the door; fill them, till they take no more."

I knew the jars were empty, all the guests washed their hands,
And some splashed their feet to get rid of the sand,
Suddenly, someone shouted, "The water has changed into wine!"
As I passed by Jesus, His eyes met mine.

I stood there listening
As jesting and laughter came from the guests,
Someone shouted, "Clever Jonas, he waited till after we dined
Before he requested the very best wine!"

Who was this man? I was troubled, burdened with sin
An inner voice said, 'Go talk with Him...'
That day, I didn't know how thankful I'd be
As I served at a wedding in sweet Galilee.

Jesus showed me compassion, loved me like a friend
One I could trust until my life ends,
Many trusted the Master, God's only Son
What will we do now, now He's dead and gone?

I know many priests said, His teaching is wrong
Yet many came secretly,
Seeking grace for their race
And many found it as they looked on His blessed face.

My Lords love and compassion must never die
There are so many believers, not just I,
His first miracle in sweet Galilee
Offered a new wine of hope to set people free.

So many like me tasted and found
The miracle of love that so freely comes,
When we trust and believe,
 In Jesus, The Christ, God's only Son.

Leave taking...

Different countries have different words for saying goodbye. I have listed just a few, 'Aloha', 'Arrivederci', 'Au Revoir', 'Auf Wiedersehen'. Regardless of the countries, these words all express the same meaning - goodbye.

In 1984 I said goodbye to my much-loved second son. He had been diagnosed with an incurable cancer in February of that year; his life expectancy was nine months. Professors said he would get weaker as the weeks passed. The opposite happened, he got stronger. Eighteen months prior to his illness he became a Christian, he and all the family thought his wellness was a tiny miracle.

All his working life was devoted to his hobby, repairing old cars. His interest suddenly changed and his main interest became the Bible. We would talk about God, Jesus, life, death and the devil, openly and without embarrassment. He knew the love and peace of God and wasn't scared if his sickness did come back. Unfortunately it did and with a vengeance.

It was hard to say goodbye to my twenty-two-year-old son and friend. Many who may be reading this and have felt the pain of loss when a loved one dies, will know how I felt.

Easter time, the next year gave me hope to face each day. As I reflected on the life and death of our Lord, recollection came to me. God in his goodness had blessed me. In the months prior to my son's death, we had talked and shared so much, we confided and crowded into those few precious months, a lifetime. God had given both of us, the gift of time and togetherness, before death parted us. Not forever, just for a little while.

I know of another mother, her name was Mary. She knew her son Jesus would be special from before His birth. We have no evidence, but we assume that for thirty years He lived at home and continued His work as a carpenter. The Bible gives us small glimpses of how much time He spent with his mother in the years before His death.

No one can express the pain and heartache of Mary as she stood watching her son die on a Roman Cross. What thoughts did she have on Crucifixion night? I, in a humble way, have tried to reach across two thousand years, to listen to Mary, the devoted mother of our Lord.

Leave Taking...

Hours ago they brought me home
"Rest now… Sleep now" they said,
Can't they see I am not here
I linger, in the ugliness of pain, His pain.

Faces, Voices, I want to cry, "Go away, go away",
Nothing matters,
Kind friends, loving friends
They cannot see, I am not here.

I am in another time, another night
A night when joy and dread shared light,
A time of words and shadows in my mind
Angel words, 'A Child to save mankind.'

That night as I touched his brow so fair
I saw no thorn, no blood-stained hair,
I kissed His smile, felt His heartbeat
I saw no pain in birth-night sleep.

Memories, year on year, all past, all gone
The learning years of a carpenter's son,
Years of a child, then too soon a man
A man of vision, a time of plans.

Leave taking...

Three summers ago we said farewell
I watched as he greeted his trusted friends,
One last wave and my tears came again
Tears for a worker of wood, and a few fishermen.

Twelve loyal men, until one without pride
Was snared, enticed by a silvery bribe… just a kiss,
A kiss they said, by the old garden gate
In return Roman coin, a traitor's rate.

It comes again, the crack, the sharp quick crack
As tails beat air then crash on back,
It comes again, the steady thud
As iron meets wood, a gush of blood.

I see again the greedy flies
On his broken brow they feed and lie,
I see the blade in the darkening sun
I hear his words, `It is over, finished, done.`

"Sleep now, rest now," dear friends plead
But sleep won't come to eyes that weep,
Dear God, I come to thee
With burdened soul and thoughts that grieve.

Almighty God, forgive my fear, my heated tear
Hold me close, draw me near,
Scatter the darkness, let it fade
From one who reasoned not, when just a maid.

Merciful Father still my soul, till in Thy time
And by Thy hand my eyes shall see,
Your Holy will, your blessed plan
That was born with a Child in Judah's land.

Loving Father, tears come again, humble tears
Tears of love and gratitude,
A mother's tears
Tears for her dearest Son... a son of thirty-three years.

Treasure...

It was that time of year again, the church jumble sale. I had been pestered, in the nicest possible way, by the various church organisations with their oft repeated cry for something for our stall. It made me think of a shelf of cuckoo clocks, some five minutes slower than the others, but all striking twelve.

The repeated appeals also brought to mind a memory from my childhood, the cry of the rag man as he made his monthly round. His appeal was slightly different, but *'Any old rags, any old rags?'* meant the same thing. Well not quite, old rags would not be accepted, what the stallholders wanted were good clothes and bric-a-brac, although in this day and age clothes are referred to as rags! My trip to the attic in search of the annual somethings loomed ahead. I wonder if you have a room where the *'must keep that, might be useful'* items spend their days, in the company of spiders and mothballs.

My jumble search took place one morning in September. In the quietness of the small room I had gathered an assortment of items; curtains that had shrunk in the wash, shoes that made blisters appear on my heels, glass ornaments and three handbags.

My search was over, until the next time! As I packed the bits and pieces, my eye caught sight of my treasure box, a box I had kept and opened many times over the years. I left the packing aside and pulled the box towards me. Gently I lifted out my tissue-wrapped treasures, and lovingly touched each item, remembering why I had kept it. My box of memories contained a part of my life and a part of my unseen heart.

The stallholders were delighted with my contribution and the sale was a success, even my glass ornament's got a home!

A few days later I was thinking of my treasure box and it brought to mind Mary the mother of Jesus. I'm sure she too, had a treasure box that she kept in her heart, memories of her life journey with God, of Jesus as a baby, a growing boy and then as a man. Perhaps like many of us, she kept her treasure hidden and like us, she could open her box anytime she wanted…

Jesus said, *'For where your treasure is, there your heart will be also.'* (Matthew 6:21)

Treasure...

Hidden in my garret high
Unnoticed by the searching eye,
A treasure trove in secret lies
My memory box of years gone by.

Behind the tight closed attic door
I spread the contents on the floor,
Once more I wander through the years
And touch the smiles, the sighs and tears.

Some photographs tinged brown with time
A battered book of nursery rhymes,
Some tiny shoes, a crochet shawl
A flowered dress on handmade doll.

A picture made with coloured string
Three tin drums that made a dim,
Postcards from a foreign land
Letters from a loved one's hand.

A wind-up box of lullabies
A china doll that sleeps and cries,
Faded ribbons tied with lace
A pair of model cars that raced.

Beside a small carved wooden boat
Tin soldiers sleep in tarnished coats,
A squeak-less duck, a cricket bat
A sheriff's badge and cowboy hat.

Treasure...

A one-eared cat that's lost its purr
A glass-eyed bear with matted fur,
Twinkling bright from small glass jar
A string of beads and a silver star.

Four baby curls in a gilded frame
Teething rings and walking reins,
Laying as they'd first been bought
A bunch of dried forget-me-nots.

With care I close the box again
And hide it in the silent den,
Concealed once more from prying eyes
My treasure trove in secret lies.

Sometime in time, I know not when
My box will open up again,
Once more I'll roam where memories lie
And touch the tears, the smiles and sighs.

JOY

First light...

When we were children, my friends and I looked forward to preparing for the first treat of the year, Easter day. Eggs would be placed in different saucepans with water and lots of tea leaves, nettles or ink. The eggs would boil for an hour or until their shells turned green, brown or blue. The following day the eggs would be painted in bright colours, then would sit like a row of Humpty-Dumpties on the sideboard, until Sunday afternoon.

On Easter day, after Sunday school and dinner we would all set out for the big park. When we arrived we were not alone, it seemed everyone in the town had the same idea! The race was on to find the *hilliest hill*.

What fun it was to see all the coloured eggs rolling down the hills, some of them would burst open as they crashed into the trees at the bottom. This was the fun part of Easter day, earlier we all had been reminded just why we rolled our eggs. The Easter story was one of sadness and joy, we all had been taught at home and in Sunday school about Good Friday and how Jesus had died, that was the sad part. The happy part was when Jesus arose from the grave on the Sunday.

This part used to have a few of us wondering why our cats and dogs that had died, couldn't be alive again too. It was a few years before we all fully understood the death and resurrection of Jesus. Children are children; as soon as the egg rolling was over we would talk of the next treat, our annual trip to the sea-side with the Sunday school!

Rolling eggs down a hill brings to mind Mary Magdalene. When she set out that morning to go to the graveyard, she was still grieving over the death of her much-loved friend. The burial ground would have been eerie with night mists still clinging to grass and trees. Perhaps Mary didn't notice her surrounding as she walked in the pale morning light. As she neared the grave, her foremost thoughts would have been on the stone at the entrance. How would she move it? Would she have the strength? All thoughts would have left her as she reached the grave - it was wide open - the stone had been rolled away.

First Light...

I hurried there in morning mist
Wondering how the stone to shift,
My footfalls quiet on the ground
The death place silent, bare of sound.

Breathless, I stopped to rest
Worried still about my quest,
Then suddenly my heart raced
Ahead the tomb, no stone in place.

I sensed someone watching me
Perhaps a gardener, clearing leaves,
Then a voice brought joy and pain.
The voice I loved, called me by name.

The Friend who cared so much for me
Slowly moved from behind a tree,
I thought, a trick, my eyes deceive
Then He stepped out in front of me.

My Lord whose life Calvary had claimed
Still bore the marks of death and shame,
Nail prints upon His hands and feet
On His dear brow thorn prints deep.

He who gave me sweet compassion
A love that knew no bounds or ration,
Was asking me to tell His friends
He was alive and back again.

How I wanted just to touch
The gentle face I loved so much,
I hesitated, loath to part
From the man who knew my soul, my heart.

With one last look upon His face
I ran quickly from that place,
Ran to find and tell His friends,
"The Master bids you come and talk again…"

Hasty words...

God told Noah to build a special boat. The Lord God gave him the measurement and stated it was to be built on a high hill. Noah obeyed. The townsfolk laughed and said, "A boat on top of a hill, Noah has lost his mind!"

Noah pleaded with the people to come aboard before the great flood came. The people laughed and teased him even more, when they saw scores of animals being herded on to the boat. Neither Noah, nor his family could persuade one person to listen to the warning.

The rains came; soon the rivers were overflowing and the land around the town was like a swamp. The people were alarmed but thought, *'it's just heavy rain.'* They still doubted Noah, until they saw with their own eyes he had been telling the truth. For them it was too late. It rained for forty days and forty nights; the boat with its eight occupants and numerous animals, drifted far from the bodies of the faithless people.

Like the towns people of Noah's day, we all have at one time or another said, "unless I see it I won't believe it." That statement and the outcome of the great flood brings to mind the disciple Thomas. Thomas loved Jesus so much; that night he was heartbroken and guilt-ridden over the death of his Master. The betrayal of Jesus by Judas Iscariot could possibility have shaken his trust in anything the other disciples said. Nothing would convince Thomas that Jesus was alive until he saw the Master standing before him.

Jesus said, *"Blessed are those who have not seen and yet have believe."* (John 20:29)

Hasty Words...

A week had passed, a week filled with misgivings
Doubt still lingered as I reached the house,
I needed to talk and remember
 My Master and Friend...

I rushed into the noisy room
Excitement filled, where was the gloom,
I listened as they joyfully said,
"Our Master lives, He is not dead!"

I sneered upon their cruel words
I'd seen Him dead... The Christ, The Lord,
How could he be alive?
Why did they jibe and tell me lies.

Angrily I turned to leave
Then came a touch upon my sleeve,
I thought they played another trick
Annoyed, I turned around so quick.

Standing there before my eyes
The Master I'd seen crucified,
I felt shame, then tears on cheek,
He had heard my disbelief.

Gently He took my hand
And laid it on His nail pierced palm,
I saw again His torn side,
And cruel marks that hair can't hide.

Hasty words…

He told me tenderly that night
Of many who will follow light,
Their faith casting doubt aside,
Believing hearts where trust abides.

As I looked again at my Masters face
I felt His love my heart embrace,
All doubt and fear cast out, overcome
By my Living Lord.. the Risen Son.

I Give Thanks...

I give thanks to God for my Bible;
I give thanks for the Saints written Word
For its there I share the life of my Saviour,
God's Son, Jesus Christ, Risen Lord.

As a baby born in a manger on a star-lit Bethlehem night,
Unaware of forth coming danger, He slept in peace that Holy Night.

As a young man with Joseph, His hands learning to cut and shape,
An apprentice to a carpenter, making chairs, tables and gates.

As a grown man who healed the sick, or tenderly blessed a child,
The healing hands of Jesus pure and undefiled.

As a dying innocent man, His hands bloodied and maimed,
His body torn and broken on the Calvary cross of shame.

As I read of the triumphant man, the risen Jesus Christ,
Who waits at heaven's door and offers Eternal Life.

I give thanks to God for the Christ Child
for the crucified man on the tree,
For the precious words in the Bible
for the truth that sets us free.

I give thanks to God my Father, for giving his Son for me...

CONTACT

If you wish to contact the author, email your request to author@MauriceWylieMedia.com

INSPIRED TO WRITE A BOOK?
Contact

Maurice Wylie Media
Inspirational Christian Publisher

Based in Northern Ireland and distributing across the world.

www.MauriceWylieMedia.com

www.ingramcontent.com/pod-product-compliance
Lightning Source LLC
Chambersburg PA
CBHW070058080526
44586CB00013B/1113